THE YEAR OF THE
CHICAGO
BLACKHAWKS®

Library and Archives Canada Cataloguing in Publication available upon request.

Published simultaneously in the United States of America by
McClelland & Stewart, a division of Random House of Canada Limited
P.O. Box 1030, Plattsburgh, New York 12901

Library of Congress Control Number: 2013943343

Printed and bound in the United States of America

Fenn/McClelland & Stewart,
a division of Random House of Canada Limited
One Toronto Street,
Toronto, Ontario
M5C 2V6
www.randomhouse.ca

1   2   3   4   5   17   16   15   14   13

THE YEAR OF THE

CHICAGO BLACKHAWKS®

2013 STANLEY CUP CHAMPIONS

OFFICIAL LICENSED PRODUCT · PRODUIT LICENCIE OFFICIEL

CELEBRATING THE 2013 STANLEY CUP CHAMPIONS

Andrew Podnieks

NHLPA™

FENN

M&S

CONTENTS

The 2012–13 Season

2013 Stanley Cup Playoffs
Conference Quarterfinals

Chicago vs. Minnesota

Chicago wins best-of-seven 4–1

Conference Semifinals

Chicago vs. Detroit

Chicago wins best-of-seven 4–3

Nothing is guaranteed until it is accomplished, so even when Chicago set an NHL record by earning points in 24 straight games to start the season and built a huge lead atop the Western Conference overall standings, those numbers meant nothing once the playoffs started. Of course, in retrospect, one might say that start meant everything and foreshadowed a great playoff run for Chicago, but such a connection can be made only after the fact.

Indeed, the Blackhawks had a great regular season, but their run in the playoffs was nothing if not filled with trials and tribulations. In the first round they beat Minnesota in five games, showing an impressive combination of offense and defense. The offense was evenly distributed through the lineup, and the defense was led by the excellent goaltending of Corey Crawford.

In the Conference Semifinals, nothing could have been less certain than the series outcome at any point of the seven games Chicago and Detroit played. Although the Blackhawks enjoyed home-ice advantage, they managed only one win in the first two games, and the Red Wings took a stranglehold on the

series by winning their first two games at the Joe Louis Arena. Improbably and incredibly, Chicago's amazing regular season seemed to be coming to an end at the hand of long-time rivals from Detroit.

But the Blackhawks fought back. They managed an impressive 4–1 win at home to make it a 3–2 series and then beat the Wings in Detroit by a much closer 4–3 score to set up a one-game showdown, winners to go on, losers to go home. Appropriately, that game went to overtime, and Brent Seabrook scored early for the Blackhawks to take the team to the next round – barely.

Now feeling the confidence and using their experience, Chicago rolled over Los Angeles, last year's Cup champions, in only five games to set up a Final against Boston. But like in the second round, the Bruins won one of the first two games at the United Center to wrest home-ice advantage away from Chicago, and won game three at home to take a 2–1 series lead.

Again, when the going got tough, Chicago got going, and the Blackhawks won Game 4 to even the series heading home. They won Game 5 at home, and

The Blackhawks rallied against Detroit; they rallied against Boston; and then, they rallied in the final minute of Game 6.

then Boston took a 2–1 lead in Game 6 late in the third, seemingly assuring fans of a Game 7.

But the Blackhawks stunned everyone by tying the game with just over a minute to go, and while everyone was getting ready for overtime, they scored again, 17 seconds later, to win the game 3–2 and win the Stanley Cup in six games. No one could have imagined this after Game 3, when the Bruins looked to be in complete control, and no one could have predicted that Boston win at home would be its last of the series.

The Blackhawks struggled at times, but when they were in a desperate situation, they played desperate hockey and came away with victory. That's experience talking, and good coaching, and smart play-making, from the scoring forwards to the checking forwards to the almost impervious defense and the great goaltending of Corey Crawford. And now, for the second time in four years, the Chicago Blackhawks are Stanley Cup champions.

A moment of sporting passion and respect as Boston's captain Zdeno Chara congratulates fellow Slovak Marian Hossa on Cup victory.

The NHL of 1925–26 consisted of seven teams, Toronto, Ottawa, two Montreal teams (Canadiens and Maroons), and three American teams, the Pittsburgh Pirates, Boston Bruins, and New York Americans. In the summer of 1926, the NHL continued its expansion into the U.S. by adding teams in Chicago and Detroit and giving New York a second team, the Rangers.

The Blackhawks were owned by Frederic McLaughlin, who had made his fortune in the coffee business but fought in World War I with the 333rd Machine Gun Battalion of the 86th Infantry Division. The 86th was nicknamed the "Blackhawk Division," and it was this connection that inspired McLaughlin to name his hockey team Black Hawks (as two words; the name changed to Blackhawks in the summer of 1986).

The Hawks played their first NHL game on November 17, 1926, at the Chicago Coliseum, beating the Toronto St. Pats (later Maple Leafs) by a 4–1 score. It wasn't until early in the 1929–30 season that the team moved into the much larger Chicago Stadium, the team's home for the next 65 years. The Stadium was known for its huge and loud pipe organ, the only one of its kind in an NHL arena and the mechanism that became world-famous for inveighing fans to cheer on their team.

Clearly a patriot, McLaughlin didn't care that he knew little about hockey or that virtually all NHL players came from Canada. He assumed the role of general manager and assembled a team with as many American players as possible. Although they were by no means an instant success, the Hawks soon became a very good hockey team, making the Stanley Cup Final in 1931 with a team led by Johnny Gottselig.

Though they lost to the Canadiens that season, goalie Charlie Gardiner was sensational three years later, leading the Hawks to a Cup win in 1934 after beating Detroit, 1–0, in double overtime of the decisive game. In 1938, the team consisted of mostly U.S.-born players and had a terrible 14–25–9 record, barely making it into the playoffs. Yet they made the most of their chance, beating both the Montreal Canadiens and New York Americans in overtime of the final game of the best-of-three series to advance to the Final. The Hawks then beat Toronto in four games of a best-of-five to win their second Cup in five seasons.

McLaughlin passed away in 1944, the year the Hawks went to the Final for the first time since 1938. They lost to the Canadiens in four straight of the now best-of-seven, and for most of the next 15 years the Hawks were among the worst in the NHL. But their fortunes changed when they signed three future great players – Bobby Hull, Stan Mikita, and Pierre Pilote – and acquired forward Ted Lindsay and goalie Glenn Hall form the Red Wings. The team quickly joined the elite, and in 1961 it won the third Stanley Cup in franchise history. They reached the Final again in 1962 and 1965 but lost to Toronto and Montreal, respectively.

After the Hawks missed the playoffs in 1968–69, they had one of the longest runs of success in professional sports, making the playoffs for 28 consecutive seasons. Early in that run they entered one of the finest eras of their history under the leadership of up-and-comers Tony Esposito in goal and Bobby Hull's younger brother, Dennis, on the wing. The Hawks advanced to the Cup final in 1971 and 1973, losing to Montreal on both occasions, however. It wasn't until 1992 that they got as far in the playoffs.

After moving into the United Center the team again went through troubled times, making the playoffs only once in ten seasons between 1997 and 2008. The franchise was rejuvenated in 2007 when Rocky Wirtz took over as team owner after his father Bill passed away.

The team's glory days of the 21st century reached its apex in the spring of 2010. Led by captain Jonathan Toews, the Hawks won the Stanley Cup by losing only six games in the now four rounds of playoff hockey necessary to win. That victory ignited a city's passion for hockey and rewarded its faithful fans for 49 years of patience. With ownership reliable and confident in its general manager, with a group of young stars still very much in the early years of their prime, and with the city excited about hockey every day of the calendar year, Chicago is once again the toast of the NHL.

Just as they called Gordie Howe Mr. Hockey, they called Chicago goalie Glenn Hall Mr. Goalie. He backstopped the team to its Stanley Cup win in 1961.

The Stadium

The earliest years of the Chicago Blackhawks saw the team play its home games out of the Chicago Coliseum, a 6,000-seat venue in downtown Chicago. The Hawks played their first NHL game there on November 17, 1926, a 4–1 win over the Toronto St. Pats. Team owner Fredric McLaughlin got into a dispute with the Coliseum owners, and when the Stadium wasn't ready in time for the 1928–29 season the Hawks were forced to play their games in Detroit and Fort Erie, Ontario for the last half of the season.

The team returned to the Coliseum under better circumstances to start 1929–30, but by the midway point of that season the Hawks moved into the Stadium. They played their first game on December 15, 1929, a 3–1 win over the Pittsburgh Pirates before a team-record crowd of 14,212. The arena last hosted an NHL game on April 28, 1994, when the visiting Toronto Maple Leafs beat Chicago, 1–0, in a playoff game.

The United Center

Although the United Center opened in the summer of 1994, it didn't host its first NHL game until 1995 because of the NHL lockout. The Blakchawks beat Edmonton, 5–1, on January 25, 1995, the first game at the United Center. Joe Murphy scored the first NHL goal at the new venue, for the home side, in the second period. The arena is still the largest for hockey in the United States. Although the official capacity is listed as 19,717, it has frequently held more than 22,000 for Blackhawks games in the last several seasons as the team has surged to the top of the attendance standings in the NHL.

The 2012–2013 Season

Because of the late start to the season there was little time to experiment and tinker with the roster. As a result, Chicago invited only 26 players to an abbreviated training camp, which started on January 14, 2013.

Invitees included only players who were mainstays from the previous season or who were newly-acquired during the off season. The chance for the coaching staff to evaluate newer talent or up-and-coming talent had to be deferred to the staff of the farm team, in Rockford of the AHL.

Player	2012–13 Status	Player	2012–13 Status
Bryan Bickell	Chicago, NHL	**Nick Leddy**	Chicago, NHL/Rockford, AHL
Dave Bolland	Chicago, NHL	**Jamal Mayers**	Chicago, NHL
Brandon Bollig	Chicago, NHL/Rockford, AHL	**Steve Montador**	Rockford, AHL
Sheldon Brookbank	Chicago, NHL/Rockford, AHL	**Johnny Oduya**	Chicago, NHL
Daniel Carcillo	Chicago, NHL	**Brandon Pirri**	Chicago, NHL/Rockford, AHL
Corey Crawford	Chicago, NHL	**Michal Rozsival**	Chicago, NHL
Ray Emery	Chicago, NHL	**Brandon Saad**	Chicago, NHL/Rockford, AHL
Michael Frolik	Chicago, NHL	**Brent Seabrook**	Chicago, NHL
Niklas Hjalmarsson	Chicago, NHL	**Patrick Sharp**	Chicago, NHL
Marian Hossa	Chicago, NHL	**Andrew Shaw**	Chicago, NHL/Rockford, AHL
Patrick Kane	Chicago, NHL	**Viktor Stalberg**	Chicago, NHL
Duncan Keith	Chicago, NHL	**Ryan Stanton**	Chicago, NHL/Rockford, AHL
Marcus Kruger	Chicago, NHL/Rockford, AHL	**Jonathan Toews**	Chicago, NHL

Duncan Keith is one of the studs of the Chicago blue-line corps.

EASTERN CONFERENCE

Atlantic	GP	W	L	OTL	GF	GA	Pts
Pittsburgh	48	36	12	0	165	119	72
NY Rangers	48	26	18	4	130	112	56
NY Islanders	48	24	17	7	139	139	55
Philadelphia	48	23	22	3	133	141	49
New Jersey	48	19	19	10	112	129	48
Northeast	GP	W	L	OTL	GF	GA	Pts
Montreal	48	29	14	5	149	126	63
Boston	48	28	14	6	131	109	62
Toronto	48	26	17	5	145	133	57
Ottawa	48	25	17	6	116	104	56
Buffalo	48	21	21	6	125	143	48
Southeast	GP	W	L	OTL	GF	GA	Pts
Washington	48	27	18	3	149	130	57
Winnipeg	48	24	21	3	128	144	51
Carolina	48	19	25	4	128	160	42
Tampa Bay	48	18	26	4	148	150	40
Florida	48	15	27	6	112	171	36

WESTERN CONFERENCE

Central	GP	W	L	OTL	GF	GA	Pts
Chicago	**48**	**36**	**7**	**5**	**155**	**102**	**77**
St. Louis	48	29	17	2	129	115	60
Detroit	48	24	16	8	124	115	56
Columbus	48	24	17	7	120	119	55
Nashville	48	16	23	9	111	139	41
Northwest	GP	W	L	OTL	GF	GA	Pts
Vancouver	48	26	15	7	127	121	59
Minnesota	48	26	19	3	122	127	55
Edmonton	48	19	22	7	125	134	45
Calgary	48	19	25	4	128	160	42
Colorado	48	16	25	7	116	152	39
Pacific	GP	W	L	OTL	GF	GA	Pts
Anaheim	48	30	12	6	140	118	66
Los Angeles	48	27	16	5	133	118	59
San Jose	48	25	16	7	124	116	57
Phoenix	48	21	18	9	125	131	51
Dallas	48	22	22	4	130	142	48

Date	Away	GF	Home	GF	Notes	Date	Away	GF	Home	GF	Notes
January 19, 2013	Blackhawks	5	Los Angeles	2		March 8, 2013	Blackhawks	2	Colorado	6	
January 20, 2013	Blackhawks	6	Phoenix	4		March 10, 2013	Edmonton	6	Blackhawks	5	
January 22, 2013	St. Louis	2	Blackhawks	3		March 14, 2013	Blackhawks	2	Columbus	1	(SO)
January 24, 2013	Blackhawks	3	Dallas	2	(Hossa 1:21 OT)	March 16, 2013	Blackhawks	8	Dallas	1	
January 26, 2013	Blackhawks	3	Columbus	2		March 18, 2013	Blackhawks	5	Colorado	2	
January 27, 2013	Detroit	1	Blackhawks	2	(Leddy 2:45 OT)	March 20, 2013	Blackhawks	2	Anaheim	4	
January 30, 2013	Blackhawks	2	Minnesota	3	(SO)	March 25, 2013	Los Angeles	5	Blackhawks	4	
February 1, 2013	Blackhawks	1	Vancouver	2	(SO)	March 26, 2013	Calgary	0	Blackhawks	2	
February 2, 2013	Blackhawks	3	Calgary	2	(SO)	March 29, 2013	Anaheim	2	Blackhawks	1	
February 5, 2013	Blackhawks	5	San Jose	3		March 31, 2013	Blackhawks	7	Detroit	1	
February 7, 2013	Blackhawks	6	Phoenix	2		April 1, 2013	Nashville	2	Blackhawks	3	(SO)
February 10, 2013	Blackhawks	3	Nashville	0		April 4, 2013	St. Louis	4	Blackhawks	3	(SO)
February 12, 2013	Anaheim	3	Blackhawks	2	(SO)	April 6, 2013	Blackhawks	1	Nashville	0	
February 15, 2013	San Jose	1	Blackhawks	4		April 7, 2013	Nashville	3	Blackhawks	5	
February 17, 2013	Los Angeles	2	Blackhawks	3		April 9, 2013	Blackhawks	1	Minnesota	0	
February 19, 2013	Vancouver	3	Blackhawks	4	(SO)	April 12, 2013	Detroit	2	Blackhawks	3	(SO)
February 22, 2013	San Jose	1	Blackhawks	2		April 14, 2013	Blackhawks	2	St. Louis	0	
February 24, 2013	Columbus	0	Blackhawks	1		April 15, 2013	Dallas	2	Blackhawks	5	
February 25, 2013	Edmonton	2	Blackhawks	3	(Hossa 1:44 OT)	April 19, 2013	Nashville	4	Blackhawks	5	(Hossa 0:52 OT)
February 28, 2013	Blackhawks	3	St. Louis	0		April 20, 2013	Phoenix	3	Blackhawks	2	(SO)
March 1, 2013	Columbus	3	Blackhawks	4	(Seabrook 3:23 OT)	April 22, 2013	Blackhawks	1	Vancouver	3	
March 3, 2013	Blackhawks	2	Detroit	1	(SO)	April 24, 2013	Blackhawks	4	Edmonton	1	
March 5, 2013	Minnesota	3	Blackhawks	5		April 26, 2013	Calgary	1	Blackhawks	3	
March 6, 2013	Colorado	2	Blackhawks	3		April 27, 2013	Blackhawks	1	St. Louis	3	

Patrick Kane led the Blackhawks in scoring during the regular season with 55 points in 47 games.

Forwards and Defensemen	GP	G	A	P	Pim
Patrick Kane	47	23	32	55	8
Jonathan Toews	47	23	25	48	27
Marian Hossa	40	17	14	31	16
Duncan Keith	47	3	24	27	31
Brandon Saad	46	10	17	27	12
Bryan Bickell	48	9	14	23	25
Viktor Stalberg	47	9	14	23	25
Patrick Sharp	28	6	14	20	14
Brent Seabrook	47	8	12	20	23
Nick Leddy	48	6	12	18	10
Andrew Shaw	48	9	6	15	38
Dave Bolland	35	7	7	14	22
Marcus Kruger	47	4	9	13	24
Michal Rozsival	27	0	12	12	14
Johnny Oduya	48	3	9	12	10
Niklas Hjalmarsson	46	2	8	10	22
Michael Frolik	45	3	7	10	8
Michal Handzus	11	1	5	6	4
Daniel Carcillo	23	2	1	3	11
Jamal Mayers	19	0	2	2	16
Sheldon Brookbank	26	1	0	1	21
Ben Smith	1	1	0	1	0
Shawn Lalonde	1	0	0	0	0
Brandon Pirri	1	0	0	0	0
Ryan Stanton	1	0	0	0	2
Brandon Bollig	25	0	0	0	51
Drew Leblanc	2	0	0	0	0

Goalies	GP	W–L–OT	Mins	GA	SO	GAA
Corey Crawford	30	19–5–5	1,761	57	3	1.94
Ray Emery	21	17–1–0	1,116	36	3	1.94
Carter Hutton	1	0–1–0	59	3	0	3.05

Goalie Corey Crawford came into his own in 2012–13 and was the number-one goalie for the Blackhawks during the playoffs.

Conference Quarterfinals

EASTERN CONFERENCE

Pittsburgh (1) vs. NY Islanders (8)

May 1	NY Islanders 0 at Pittsburgh 5 [Fleury]
May 3	NY Islanders 4 at Pittsburgh 3
May 5	Pittsburgh 5 at NY Islanders 4 (Kunitz 8:44 OT)
May 7	Pittsburgh 4 at NY Islanders 6
May 9	NY Islanders 0 at Pittsburgh 4 [Vokoun]
May 11	Pittsburgh 4 at NY Islanders 3 (Orpik 7:49 OT)

Pittsburgh wins best-of-seven 4–2

Montreal (2) vs. Ottawa (7)

May 2	Ottawa 4 at Montreal 2
May 3	Ottawa 1 at Montreal 3
May 5	Montreal 1 at Ottawa 6
May 7	Montreal 2 at Ottawa 3 (Turris 2:32 OT)
May 9	Ottawa 6 at Montreal 1

Ottawa wins best-of-seven 4–1

Washington (3) vs. NY Rangers (6)

May 2	NY Rangers 1 at Washington 3
May 4	NY Rangers 0 at Washington 1 (Green 8:00 OT) [Holtby]
May 6	Washington 3 at NY Rangers 4
May 8	Washington 3 at NY Rangers 4
May 10	NY Rangers 1 at Washington 2 (Ribeiro 9:24 OT)
May 12	Washington 0 at NY Rangers 1 [Lundqvist]
May 13	NY Rangers 5 at Washington 0 [Lundqvist]

NY Rangers win best-of-seven 4–3

Boston (4) vs. Toronto (5)

May 1	Toronto 1 at Boston 4
May 4	Toronto 4 at Boston 2
May 6	Boston 5 at Toronto 2
May 8	Boston 4 at Toronto 3 (Krejci 13:06 OT)
May 10	Toronto 2 at Boston 1
May 12	Boston 1 at Toronto 2
May 13	Toronto 4 at Boston 5 (Bergeron 6:05 OT)

Boston wins best-of-seven 4–3

WESTERN CONFERENCE

Chicago (1) vs. Minnesota (8)

April 30	Minnesota 1 at Chicago 2 (Bickell 16:35 OT)
May 3	Minnesota 2 at Chicago 5
May 5	Chicago 2 at Minnesota 3 (Zucker 2:15 OT)
May 7	Chicago 3 at Minnesota 0 [Crawford]
May 9	Minnesota 1 at Chicago 5

Chicago wins best-of-seven 4–1

Anaheim (2) vs. Detroit (7)

April 30	Detroit 1 at Anaheim 3
May 2	Detroit 5 at Anaheim 4 (Nyqvist 1:21 OT)
May 4	Anaheim 4 at Detroit 0 [Hiller]
May 6	Anaheim 2 at Detroit 3 (Brunner 15:10 OT)
May 8	Detroit 2 at Anaheim 3 (Bonino 1:54 OT)
May 10	Anaheim 3 at Detroit 4 (Zetterberg 1:04 OT)
May 12	Detroit 3 at Anaheim 2

Detroit wins best-of-seven 4–3

Vancouver (3) vs. San Jose (6)

May 1	San Jose 3 at Vancouver 1
May 3	San Jose 3 at Vancouver 2 (Torres 5:31 OT)
May 5	Vancouver 2 at San Jose 5
May 7	Vancouver 3 at San Jose 4 (Marleau 13:18 OT)

San Jose wins best-of-seven 4–0

St. Louis (4) vs. Los Angeles (5)

April 30	Los Angeles 1 at St. Louis 2 (Steen 13:26 OT)
May 2	Los Angeles 1 at St. Louis 2
May 4	St. Louis 0 at Los Angeles 1 [Quick]
May 6	St. Louis 3 at Los Angeles 4
May 8	Los Angeles 3 at St. Louis 2 (Voynov 8:00 OT)
May 10	St. Louis 1 at Los Angeles 2

Los Angeles wins best-of-seven 4–2

Conference Semifinals

EASTERN CONFERENCE

Pittsburgh (1) vs. Ottawa (7)

May 14	Ottawa 1 at Pittsburgh 4
May 17	Ottawa 3 at Pittsburgh 4
May 19	Pittsburgh 1 at Ottawa 2 (Greening 27:39 OT)
May 22	Pittsburgh 7 at Ottawa 3
May 24	Ottawa 2 at Pittsburgh 6

Pittsburgh wins best-of-seven 4–1

Boston (4) vs. NY Rangers (6)

May 16	NY Rangers 2 at Boston 3 (Marchand 15:40 OT)
May 19	NY Rangers 2 at Boston 5
May 21	Boston 2 at NY Rangers 1
May 23	Boston 3 at NY Rangers 4 (Kreider 7:03 OT)
May 25	NY Rangers 1 at Boston 3

Boston wins best-of-seven 4–1

WESTERN CONFERENCE

Chicago (1) vs. Detroit (7)

May 15	Detroit 1 at Chicago 4
May 18	Detroit 4 at Chicago 1
May 20	Chicago 1 at Detroit 3
May 23	Chicago 0 at Detroit 2 [Howard]
May 25	Detroit 1 at Chicago 4
May 27	Chicago 4 at Detroit 3
May 29	Detroit 1 at Chicago 2 (Seabrook 3:35 OT)

Chicago wins best-of-seven 4–3

Los Angeles (5) vs. San Jose (6)

May 14	San Jose 0 at Los Angeles 2 [Quick]
May 16	San Jose 3 at Los Angeles 4
May 18	Los Angeles 1 at San Jose 2 (Couture 1:29 OT)
May 21	Los Angeles 1 at San Jose 2
May 23	San Jose 0 at Los Angeles 3 [Quick]
May 26	Los Angeles 1 at San Jose 2
May 28	San Jose 1 at Los Angeles 2

Los Angeles wins best-of-seven 4–3

Conference Finals

EASTERN CONFERENCE

Pittsburgh (1) vs. Boston (4)

June 1	Boston 3 at Pittsburgh 0 [Rask]
June 3	Boston 6 at Pittsburgh 1
June 5	Pittsburgh 1 at Boston 2 (Bergeron 35:19 OT)
June 7	Pittsburgh 0 at Boston 1 [Rask]

Boston wins best-of-seven 4–0

WESTERN CONFERENCE

Chicago (1) vs. Los Angeles (5)

June 1	Los Angeles 1 at Chicago 2
June 2	Los Angeles 2 at Chicago 4
June 4	Chicago 1 at Los Angeles 3
June 6	Chicago 3 at Los Angeles 2
June 8	Los Angeles 3 at Chicago 4 (Kane 31:40 OT)

Chicago wins best-of-seven 4–1

Stanley Cup Final

Chicago (1) vs. Boston (4)

June 12	Boston 3 at Chicago 4 (Shaw 52:08 OT)
June 15	Boston 2 at Chicago 1 (Paille 13:48 OT)
June 17	Chicago 0 at Boston 2 [Rask]
June 19	Chicago 6 at Boston 5 (Seabrook 9:51 OT)
June 22	Boston 1 at Chicago 3
June 24	Chicago 3 at Boston 2

Chicago wins best-of-seven 4–2

	GP	G	A	P	Pim
Patrick Kane	23	9	10	19	8
Bryan Bickell	23	9	8	17	14
Patrick Sharp	23	10	6	16	8
Marian Hossa	22	7	9	16	2
Jonathan Toews	23	3	11	14	18
Duncan Keith	22	2	11	13	18
Michal Handzus	23	3	8	11	6
Michael Frolik	23	3	7	10	6
Andrew Shaw	23	5	4	9	35
Johnny Oduya	23	3	5	8	16
Dave Bolland	18	3	3	6	24
Brandon Saad	23	1	5	6	4
Marcus Kruger	23	3	2	5	2
Niklas Hjalmarsson	23	0	5	5	4
Brent Seabrook	23	3	1	4	4
Michal Rozsival	23	0	4	4	16
Viktor Stalberg	19	0	3	3	6
Nick Leddy	23	0	2	2	4
Daniel Carcillo	4	0	1	1	6
Brandon Bollig	5	0	0	0	2
Ben Smith	1	0	0	0	0
Sheldon Brookbank	1	0	0	0	0

Brent Seabrook (left) and Duncan Keith have been one of the top defensive pairings in the NHL over the last several years.

In Goal	GP	W–L	Mins	GA	SO	GAA
Corey Crawford	23	16–7	1,504	46	1	1.84

By Draft

Bryan Bickell
Drafted 41st overall in 2004

Dave Bolland
Drafted 32nd overall in 2004

Corey Crawford
Drafted 52rd overall in 2003

Niklas Hjalmarsson
Drafted 108th overall in 2005

Patrick Kane
Drafted 1st overall in 2007

Duncan Keith
Drafted 54th overall in 2002

Marcus Kruger
Drafted 149th overall in 2009

Shawn Lalonde
Drafted 68th overall in 2008

Brandon Pirri
Drafted 59th overall in 2009

Brandon Saad
Drafted 43rd overall in 2011

Brent Seabrook
Drafted 14th overall in 2003

Andrew Shaw
Drafted 139th overall in 2011

Ben Smith
Drafted 169th overall in 2008

Jonathan Toews
Drafted 3rd overall in 2006

By Free Agent Signing

Brandon Bollig
Signed as a free agent on April 3, 2010

Sheldon Brookbank
Signed as a free agent on July 1, 2012

Daniel Carcillo
Signed as a free agent on July 1, 2011

Ray Emery
Signed as a free agent on October 3, 2011

Michael Frolik
Signed as a free agent on July 15, 2011

Marian Hossa
Signed as a free agent on July 1, 2009

Carter Hutton
Signed as a free agent on February 23, 2012

Drew Leblanc
Signed as a free agent on April 12, 2013

Jamal Mayers
Signed as a free agent on July 1, 2011

Michal Rozsival
Signed as a free agent on September 11, 2012

Ryan Stanton
Signed as a free agent on March 12, 2010

By Trade

Michal Handzus
Acquired on April 1, 2013 from San Jose for a 4th-round draft choice in 2013

Nick Leddy
Acquired on February 12, 2010 with Kim Johnsson from Minnesota for Cam Barker

Johnny Oduya
Acquired on February 27, 2012 from Winnipeg for a 2nd- and 3rd-round draft choice in 2013

Patrick Sharp
Acquired on December 5, 2005 with Eric Meloche from Philadelphia for Matt Ellison and a 3rd-round draft choice in 2006

Viktor Stalberg
Acquired on June 30, 2010 with Philippe Paradis and Chris DiDomenico from Toronto for Kris Versteeg and Bill Sweatt

ON THE FARM – ROCKFORD ICEHOGS (AHL)

Forwards and Defensemen	GP	G	A	P	Pim
Brandon Pirri	76	22	53	75	72
Martin St. Pierre	76	26	33	59	59
Ben Smith	54	27	20	47	13
Adam Clendening	73	9	37	46	67
Kyle Beach	66	16	10	26	204
Maxime Sauve	8	1	2	3	4
Ryan Stanton	73	3	22	25	126
Shawn Lalonde	59	5	18	23	91
Marcus Kruger	34	8	14	22	24
Brandon Saad	31	8	12	20	10
Rostislav Olesz	14	7	12	19	4
Brad Mills	33	7	9	16	60
Nick Leddy	31	3	13	16	12
Andrew Shaw	28	8	6	14	84
Mathieu Beaudoin	21	1	3	4	8
Terry Broadhurst	31	5	8	13	12
Brandon Svendsen	40	6	6	12	14
Peter LeBlanc	34	4	8	12	15
Dylan Olsen	50	2	9	11	27
Brett Lebda	27	0	11	11	18
Brandon Bollig	35	5	4	9	157
Ben Youds	23	1	8	9	22
Joe Lavin	39	1	8	9	16
Philippe Paradis	36	1	7	8	100
Klas Dahlbeck	70	1	5	6	29
Kenndal McArdle	30	3	2	5	55
Rob Flick	51	3	2	5	97
Steve Montador	14	2	3	5	13
David Gilbert	10	1	2	3	6
Joakim Nordstrom	11	0	3	3	12
Byron Froese	9	0	2	2	4
Carter Hutton	51	0	2	2	17
Wade Brookbank	28	0	1	1	100
Mickey Lang	1	0	0	0	0
Adam Hobson	2	0	0	0	0
Garret Ross	2	0	0	0	5
Kent Simpson	2	0	0	0	0
Kevin Quick	3	0	0	0	0
Phillip Danault	5	0	0	0	2
Mark McNeill	5	0	0	0	0
Alec Richards	11	0	0	0	0
Henrik Karlsson	18	0	0	0	12

Goalies	GP	W–L–SOL	Mins	GA	SO	GAA
Carter Hutton	51	26–22–1	2,908	132	2	2.72
Henrik Karlsson	18	11–5–0	1,007	48	0	2.86
Kent Simpson	2	1–1–0	98	5	0	3.07
Alec Richards	11	4–5–0	548	32	0	3.50

A 2009 draft choice by the Blackhawks, Brandon Pirri led the farm team in scoring in 2012–13.

GAME ONE — *APRIL 30, 2013*

Minnesota 1 at **Chicago 2** (Bickell 16:35 OT)
Chicago leads series 1–0

Chicago kicked off its quest for its first Stanley Cup since 2010 on the right note. Firing 37 shots on goal, the Western Conference's top-seeded team saw Bryan Bickell emerge as the hero with an electrifying overtime goal.

Blackhawks defenseman Johnny Oduya got the puck in the corner and flipped it high into the neutral zone, where Viktor Stalberg carried it in over the blue line. Stalberg spotted Bickell speeding to the goal and fed him perfectly in front. Bickell's backhand deke found the back of the net with 3:25 left in the first overtime, sending the United Center crowd into a frenzy.

"I was kind of . . . I don't want to say, 'cheating,' [but]

I was taking a little bit of a gamble," Bickell said. "I saw it was a high flip and then it made it over [Minnesota defenseman Ryan Suter's] glove. I knew [Stalberg] was going to get it and it was just a read on the ice to jump into the play and get that opportunity."

Chicago, which scored 155 goals in the regular season (second only to Pittsburgh's 165), had to be patient all night against the defensive-minded Wild.

The Blackhawks overcame a stellar performance by Minnesota goalie Josh Harding, who was the surprise starter after Niklas Backstrom was injured during pregame warmups. It was Harding's first start since January 30.

Chicago faced adversity in the early going. Cal Clutterbuck opened the scoring for the Wild with a wrist shot from the left side that surprised Chicago netminder Corey Crawford at 4:48 of the first period. It was Clutterbuck's first career playoff goal.

Goalie Corey Crawford peers through traffic to keep his eyes on a Minnesota shot.

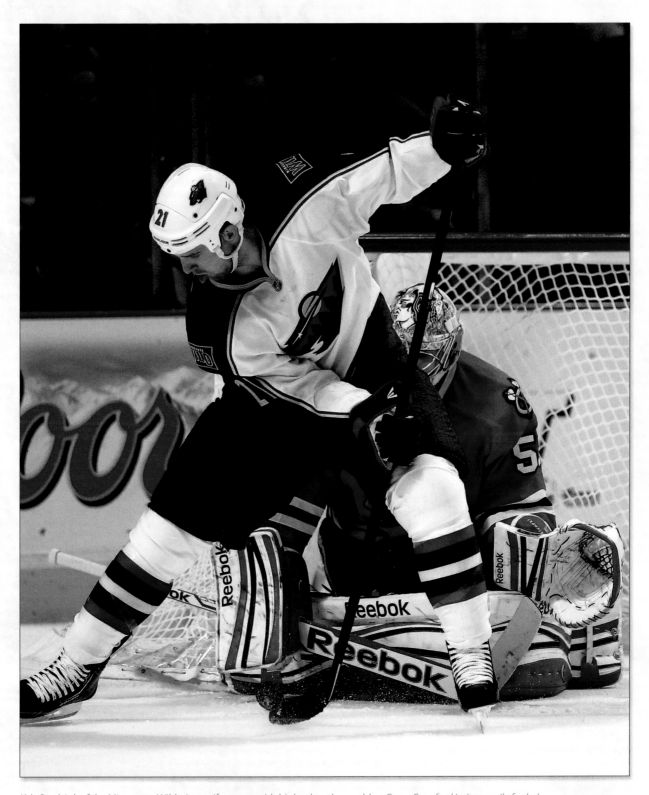

Kyle Brodziak of the Minnesota Wild tries a nifty move with his back to the goal, but Corey Crawford isn't so easily fooled.

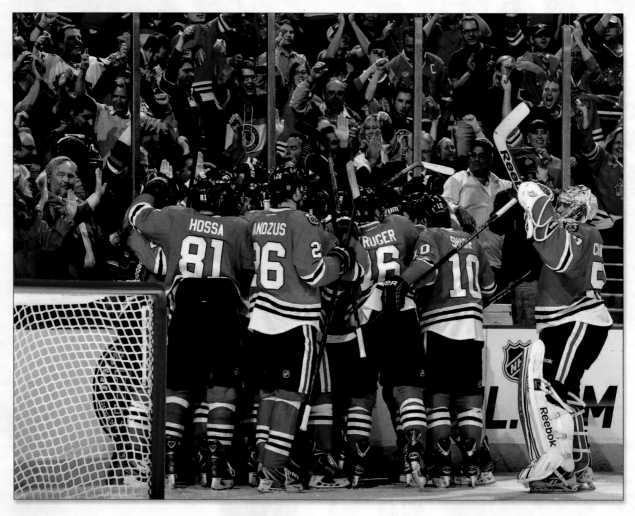

The Blackhawks mob Bryan Bickell after he scored the overtime winner in Game 1.

"It's not the way I wanted to start, but I was able to regroup pretty well," Crawford said. "The guys were behind me, encouraging me, and we played a good game. They're a tough team. They just sit around and try to take away as [many] chances from us as they can. That was a crazy one."

Crawford showed excellent form in the final minute of the first period, twice denying Kyle Brodziak from close range.

Chicago answered back with the man advantage early in the second period. Patrick Kane dipsy-doodled his way over the blue line and sent a gorgeous backhand feed past two Wild defenders to Marian Hossa in the left faceoff circle. The Slovak sniper made no mistake, zinging a wrister past Harding to tie it up at 2:06.

Chicago thought it had taken the lead halfway through the third period when captain Jonathan Toews popped the puck in during a goal-mouth scramble, but the goal didn't count because the whistle had already blown play dead as the puck was out of sight and under the Wild's Jared Spurgeon. Still, Bickell's OT heroics made the non-goal moot.

GAME TWO — MAY 3, 2013

Minnesota 2 at Chicago 5

Chicago leads series 2–0

From Bobby Hull to Denis Savard to Jeremy Roenick, the Chicago Blackhawks have always boasted top offensive talent. This year's team had as much fire-power as any of its predecessors, and that was evident in a 5–2 win over the Wild, which gave Chicago a 2–0 lead in its first-round series.

Michal Frolik and Patrick Sharp each scored twice to lead the Chicago attack. The high-flying Blackhawks peppered Minnesota goalie Josh Harding with 47 shots, while at the other end, Corey Crawford contin-ued his solid play, facing 28 shots. In the first period alone, the shots favored the Blackhawks, 17–6.

"There was big emphasis on that, to play well in the first [period], and I think we did that," said forward Patrick Kane. "There was a lot of talk about that, to get the pace going and to pick it up from where it was in Game 1 because I don't think we liked our pace in Game 1. That first period kind of set the tone."

The home team wasn't dissuaded when Kane had a first-period goal immediately waved off for kicking in the rebound from a Duncan Keith wrister. Frolik drew first blood for Chicago when Andrew Shaw's shot on the rush deflected to him at the bottom of the left faceoff circle, and he put it home at 8:34.

Another fortuitous deflection led to Frolik's 2–0 goal. Playing shorthanded at the start of the second period, the Blackhawks entered the Wild's zone and Frolik dished the puck to Keith. The former Norris

Michael Frolik puts the finishing touches on his second-period goal.

Chicago's Brandon Bollig checks Jonas Brodin in what was a physical and intense Game 2.

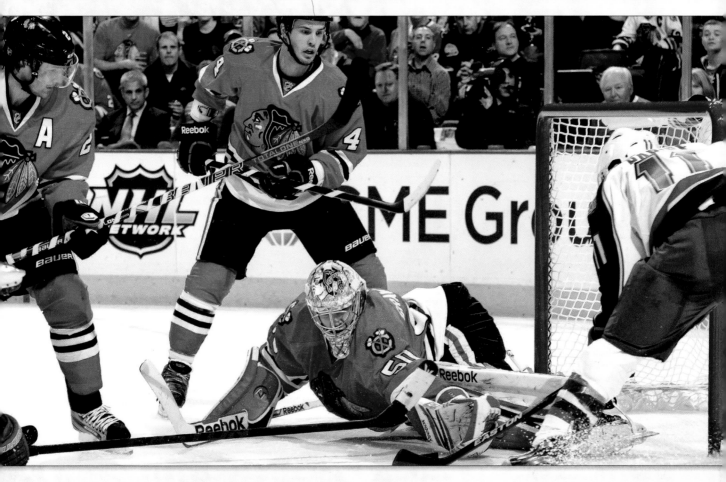

Goalie Corey Crawford was at his acrobatic best when he had to be.

Trophy winner tried a backhander that went off a Wild player and came straight back to Frolik. The Czech forward promptly scored from the slot, just 49 seconds into the middle period.

"I did not have that many [good bounces] in the season, kind of lucky bounces, and it's nice to sometimes have those bounces," said Frolik. "Always when you score some goals, the confidence goes a little higher. Hopefully it's going to help me in the next few games and I can build on that."

The Wild cut the deficit to 2–1 with 2:03 left in the second period. Matt Cullen found Devin Setoguchi streaking toward the net behind the defense, and Setoguchi snapped the puck high past Crawford's glove.

But two third-period goals by Sharp quelled Minnesota's hopes of a comeback. The veteran winger grabbed the puck on the goal line and put a quick backhand inside Harding's left post at 3:44. Then, at 14:08, Sharp was the beneficiary of Kane's brilliant stickhandling in the slot; all he had to do was bang the puck into an open net after the young American superstar eluded three Minnesota defenders and set up Sharp in the left faceoff circle.

"It's kind of a big goal to put us up two there in the third," said Sharp. "It felt good, and hopefully it's the start of many more."

Minnesota defenseman Marco Scandella scored his first career playoff goal with 3:31 left, beating Crawford through traffic to make it 4–2. But it was too little, too late. Bryan Bickell, the overtime hero in Game 1, rounded out the scoring with an empty-netter at 19:49.

Home-ice advantage had proven to be just that for Chicago, who did what they had to do before their own fans and now traveled to Minnesota for two games.

GAME THREE — MAY 5, 2013
Chicago 2 at Minnesota 3 (Zucker 2:15 OT)
Chicago leads series 2–1

For the second time in this first-round series, overtime was required to settle matters, but this time the Wild emerged victorious over the Blackhawks. Early in the first extra period, rookie Jason Zucker stunned Chicago with a nice one-timer set up by Matt Cullen from behind the goal line.

Zucker, raised in Las Vegas, enjoyed better luck than he had in Game 1, when he rang a shot off the crossbar in overtime. The 21-year-old said it all came down to making a consistent effort.

"You never deserve anything; you've always got to work for everything," Zucker said. "I just tried keeping the puck on net, and this one happened to go in for me."

Outshooting the Blackhawks, 37–27, the Wild forced the Western Conference leaders to realize they would need to elevate their game to be successful in the series. Minnesota put Chicago back on its heels with an intense physical approach.

"They got some momentum off the power play, got some zone time," said Chicago coach Joel Quenneville of the Wild. "This was the one game where we were in our zone a lot more than we would have liked to have been."

Johnny Oduya gave Chicago the start it wanted at 13:26. The Swedish-born blueliner accepted a slick cross-ice feed from Patrick Kane in the left faceoff circle and sent a wrister past Minnesota goalie Josh Harding.

But Pierre-Marc Bouchard got the equalizer for Minnesota late in the first period. After rushing the puck into the Chicago end, he went to the net and

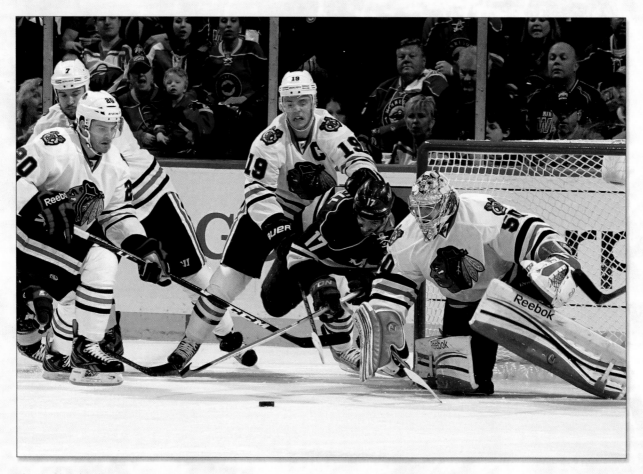

The Blackhawks were under siege in Game 3, but the score was close thanks to fine goaltending from Corey Crawford.

Playing at home for the first time, Minnesota brought another level of intensity to the rink that Chicago couldn't handle on this night, losing 3–2 in overtime.

backhanded a loose puck past Corey Crawford at 18:30, delighting the Wild faithful at Xcel Energy Center.

Following a scoreless second period, Minnesota took a 2–1 lead early in the third. Charlie Coyle sent a lovely pass from behind the net to Zach Parise out front. Parise showed the skill and focus that inspired the Wild to sign him to a long-term deal in 2012, as he flipped home a backhand at 3:09 with the calm and cool of a superstar.

Duncan Keith scored the equalizer for Chicago with 2:46 remaining. Kane played the set-up man again, finding his defenseman cruising into the left faceoff circle. Keith then hammered a slap shot past Harding.

It was Minnesota's first playoff victory since beating the Colorado Avalanche, 3–2, in overtime on April 14, 2008. Despite losing, the Blackhawks found some consolation in Crawford's excellent play between the pipes.

"He made a lot of big saves for us all game long," Keith said. "He was our best player tonight."

Chicago captain Jonathan Toews felt his team would have to change its approach to prevail in Game 4 on the road.

"You can't go out there and try to make pretty plays," said Toews. "It's got to be ugly. We're not doing that enough. Once we start doing that, we've got the strength, the speed and the skill to get on the board and make things happen."

Chicago forward Andrew Shaw makes life miserable for defenseman Ryan Suter, who tries to give his goalie a clear sight line of the puck.

GAME FOUR — *MAY 7, 2013*

Chicago 3 at Minnesota 0

Chicago leads series 3–1

Sometimes a goalie stands on his head to earn a shutout, while on other occasions he's simply as solid as his teammates.

Corey Crawford earned his second career NHL playoff shutout by blanking Minnesota, but he was quick to credit his fellow Blackhawks. And it was well-deserved credit he offered. Patrick Sharp had his second two-goal outing of the series, while Bryan Bickell scored his third goal. The whole group played well in front of Crawford, who also did what he had to do to preserve the shutout and victory.

"We just go about our business. We've had that calm, collective confidence all year long," Crawford said. "I think we definitely showed that tonight."

Particularly impressive was Chicago's penalty killing. On another night, lack of discipline might have hurt the Blackhawks. Just 1:06 into the game, Michal Handzus received an interference penalty while defending against Zach Parise, and that set the pattern. Chicago would take six minors altogether, but killed each one off with impressive resolve.

"I thought the penalty kill was outstanding," Blackhawks coach Joel Quenneville said. "It starts with the goaltender in those situations. Six [penalties] isn't a normal number for us; two or three is usually our quota. Just an outstanding job blocking shots, getting clears. I commend them for doing an outstanding job."

Marian Hossa celebrates one of Chicago's three goals in Game 4.

Goalie Josh Harding stops Jonathan Toews on a close-range opportunity.

It was a tough opening period for the Wild. They surrendered the first goal when Marian Hossa took the puck away inside the Minnesota blue line and sent a deft centering pass to Handzus. His quick release was tipped in by Sharp, standing in front, at 8:48.

Then things got worse. With less than five minutes remaining in the first, Wild goalie Josh Harding suffered a lower-body injury when Jonathan Toews tried unsuccessfully to charge to the net and deke past him.

The Chicago captain fell on Harding's left leg in the attempt.

Although Harding continued to play, he was replaced by third-stringer Darcy Kuemper to start the second period. Minnesota had already lost its top goalie, Niklas Backstrom, to an injury prior to Game 1, and he was not yet ready to return to the lineup.

Kuemper, a former Western Hockey League star with the Red Deer Rebels, didn't start the way he would have liked to his first NHL playoff game. The 23-year-old allowed a goal on the first shot he faced. Coming from Sharp at the top of the left faceoff circle, it squeaked past defenseman Jared Spurgeon and under Kuemper's stick arm. That made it 2–0 Blackhawks at 1:02.

Bickell gave Chicago some breathing space, coming out of the corner and firing a bad-angle wrister to the top shelf, over Kuemper's glove, with 7:14 remaining. That made the score an insurmountable 3–0. That was all the Blackhawks needed to take a 3–1 series stranglehold in this pivotal fourth game as teams headed back to Chicago.

A noteworthy sidebar was the play of Duncan Keith. Most men would be too exhausted to play top-level pro sports after attending the birth of their first child and barely sleeping in the process. But not Keith. The Blackhawks' alternate captain flew back to the Windy City to be with his wife, Kelly-Rae, when their son was born, and then zoomed back to Minnesota for Game 4. The hard-nosed rearguard logged a team-leading 23:57 in the victory.

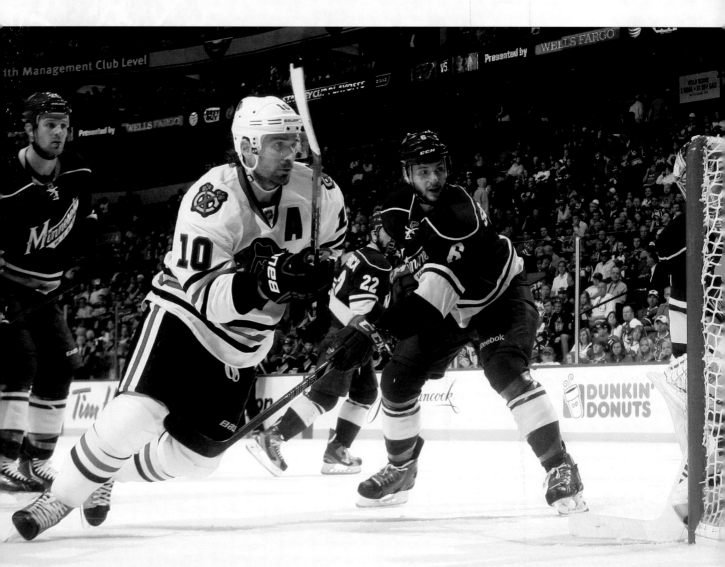

Patrick Sharp races behind the net to try to corral a loose puck.

GAME FIVE — MAY 9, 2013

Minnesota 1 at **Chicago 5**

Chicago wins series 4–1

Could the Blackhawks close out the eighth-seeded Wild on home ice and move on to the second round? Propelled by a two-goal, three-point performance by winger Marian Hossa, Chicago answered that question with an emphatic "Yes!"

Remarkably, it was the first time coach Joel Quenneville's crew had won a playoff series since defeating the Philadelphia Flyers in six games for the 2010 Stanley Cup. But despite advancing, Quenneville felt his team still had plenty of work to do.

"I think we still have to get a different type of pace to our game that's catching up to the other series that are being played and what the playoffs are all about," Quenneville said. "It's not the regular season. There's another appetite that we have to get, as well."

Chicago built a commanding 3–0 lead before the midway point of Game 5. Hossa got the game's first goal at 15:39 on a snap shot set up by Jonathan Toews – the first point of the playoffs for the captain.

In the second period, Marcus Kruger tallied on a wraparound at 3:19, stuffing the puck through Josh Harding's pads. Hossa's 3–0 goal came on a close-range backhander at 6:26.

Patrick Sharp (foreground) and Jonathan Toews celebrate a goal in Game 5.

The Wild put up a valiant fight in Game 5 but ultimately were no match for the explosive offense of the Blackhawks.

That marker ended Harding's evening, and he was replaced for the second straight game by Darcy Kuemper. However, no matter which team you were cheering for, you had to applaud Harding's valiant efforts as he'd missed a good chunk of the regular season bahe had missed a chunk of the regular season while battling side effects from medication for his multiple sclerosis.

Torrey Mitchell gave the Wild a little hope with a quick release that beat Corey Crawford from the slot just past the halfway mark. But Andrew Shaw restored Chicago's three-goal lead 35 seconds later when he capitalized on a nifty pass from Bryan Bickell and put the puck in the open side.

At 6:04 of the third period, Sharp rounded out the scoring on the power play, picking up the rebound after some excellent puck movement led to a Hossa blast. For the fifth time, the red-clad Blackhawks fans partied to their goal song, "Chelsea Dagger" by The Fratellis.

Even though the score was lopsided, Crawford had to make some tough stops, particularly in the first period. He answered critics who thought he couldn't get the job done after falling short the year before in the playoffs against the Phoenix Coyotes.

"I put it behind me, but there were definitely things I took with me from last year, whether it [was] mistakes I made or good stuff I did," Crawford acknowledged. "You always want to learn from your mistakes, and that's the only way you can get better. In certain situations, I definitely learned from last year, and it helped me this year."

When the game ended, Chicago had to wait to find out its second-round opponent.

"It doesn't matter who it's going to be," Toews said. "It's going to be a tough opponent. We can expect that much and prepare ourselves the best we can for whatever might come the second round."

Players go through the traditional handshake after Chicago eliminated Minnesota in five games.

GAME ONE — *MAY 15, 2013*

Detroit 1 at **Chicago 4**
Chicago leads 1–0

After ousting the Minnesota Wild in five games, the Blackhawks knew it wasn't going to get any easier against the Red Wings. Persistence paid off as Chicago overcame a fine 38-save performance by Detroit goalie Jimmy Howard to win the series opener, 4–1.

How formidable was Chicago's second-round opponent? Led by captain Henrik Zetterberg, the Red Wings reeled off four straight wins to earn seventh place in the Western Conference and then eliminated the Anaheim Ducks in seven games in the opening round.

The Blackhawks would have to use their speed and relentless forechecking to their advantage against the Red Wings, and that's what they did in Game 1.

"I thought it was our best game of the playoffs, no question," said Patrick Sharp, who rounded out the scoring with an empty-netter with 49 seconds left and finished with three points on the night.

The Blackhawks only had six shots in the first period, but picked up their tempo in the final 40 minutes to secure the win. Marian Hossa opened the scoring for Chicago, one-timing a nice Jonathan Toews set-up from the slot at 9:03.

"It's the type of game we like to play. The intensity was there tonight," Hossa said. "We felt like we had the fast game. We didn't hesitate with the puck, and we put it in good areas. We have a good-skating team and we used that to our advantage."

Less than two minutes after Hossa's goal, Swiss forward Damien Brunner tied it up for Detroit, tapping home the rebound from a Gustav Nyquist shot at the side of the net.

After a scoreless second period, Johnny Oduya got the eventual winner for the home side when he came in from the blue line unimpeded to take a pass from

The Blackhawks won Game 1 by a 4–1 score, but would need seven games to dispatch the Red Wings.

Conference Semifinals – Chicago Blackhawks vs. Detroit Red Wings

37

Detroit goalie Jimmy Howard keeps his eye on the puck despite heavy traffic in front of his crease.

Sharp. Oduya zinged a hard shot in off the crossbar at 8:02 of the third to make it 2–1 Chicago.

Fellow Swede Marcus Kruger gave the Blackhawks a 3–1 edge three minutes later, finding a loose puck during a goalmouth scramble and lifting a backhand over a fallen Howard at 11:23.

The score would have been more lopsided had it not been for the Detroit netminder. Howard made sensational glove saves on Brent Seabrook and Patrick Kane and foiled Dave Bolland on a breakaway. The Blackhawks had to stick with their game plan, and it paid dividends.

"I just think we've been doing it all season," said Sharp. "We've been playing the same way whether we're up a goal or down a goal, tied game, and we're not surprised with how well Jimmy is playing in net there. We're not surprised how hard it is to get to the net and get scoring chances. There's no reason to panic and no reason to change anything – just keep playing."

"I think in the first it was pretty even, but then I think in the second and third, they looked like they had a little more energy than we did," Zetterberg conceded.

The Blackhawks had set the right tone in Game 1, but this series was far from over.

Dave Bolland's close-in chance is stymied by goalie Jimmy Howard.

Conference Semifinals – Chicago Blackhawks vs. Detroit Red Wings

GAME TWO — *MAY 18, 2013*

Detroit 4 at **Chicago 1**

Series tied 1–1

Talk about turning the tables. Apart from the 4–1 final score, the only resemblance between Game 2 and Game 1 was that Chicago scored first and Damien Brunner notched the tying goal for Detroit. After that, the Red Wings taught the Blackhawks a valuable lesson in puck possession en route to equalizing the series.

"They controlled the puck a lot and we didn't, so they kind of used our own game against us playing puck possession, keeping it in [our end], and I thought we were chasing it all game," Chicago's Patrick Kane said. "By no means is it going to be an easy series or a cakewalk."

Kane got Chicago on the board at 14:05 of the first period when he one-timed a short pass from Michal Handzus on an odd-man rush, energizing the United Center crowd with the game's opening goal.

But Brunner's neat tip of a Jakub Kindl point shot at 2:05 of the second period put Detroit back on even terms. And from that point on, the Red Wings' domination only increased.

"We knew they were going to come back and try to make up for Game 1," said Chicago captain Jonathan Toews. "We didn't quite match their effort. It was frustrating, but at the same time we did a lot of good things and started getting more traffic later in the

Despite the best efforts of Corey Crawford, Detroit won Game 2 by a 4–1 score to gain home-ice advantage.

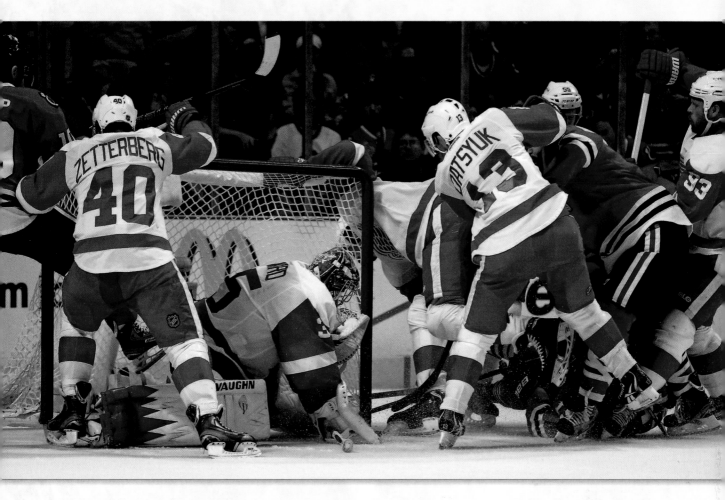

The Blackhawks managed only 20 shots all game against Jimmy Howard in Game 2.

game. We've just got to find more ways to be effective in their zone."

Detroit took a 2–1 lead at 16:08 of the second period thanks to a beautiful pass by captain Henrik Zetterberg, who recorded his first of two assists. "Z" skated down the left wing behind the Chicago net and sent the puck in front to pinching defenseman Brendan Smith, who zipped a quick shot past helpless netminder Corey Crawford.

"I think that's what makes Toews and [Pavel] Datsyuk and Zetterberg different from other guys in the League. That's what they do; they compete, and when it doesn't go their way they dig down and find a way to go harder," Detroit coach Mike Babcock said. "That's why you want them around. They are a great example for the rest of the group."

Johan Franzen counted Detroit's third goal at 7:19 of the third, accepting a long pass from Jonathan Ericsson and racing past Chicago's Niklas Hjalmarsson to beat Crawford with a great shot under the crossbar.

Less than five minutes later, Zetterberg made a clever drop pass for Valtteri Filppula inside the Chicago line, and the Finnish forward powered his way to the net and sent a backhand through Crawford's legs to make it 4–1.

The Red Wings defended effectively until the final buzzer, claiming home-ice advantage leading up to Game Three at Joe Louis Arena. Detroit outshot Chicago, 30–20.

"I wouldn't say it's a wake-up call," said Toews. "I think we know exactly what we need to improve on, and we need to do it right away." But as it turned out, there would be more learning experiences ahead for the Blackhawks.

Conference Semifinals – Chicago Blackhawks vs. Detroit Red Wings

41

Chicago's Brandon Saad is unceremoniously dumped into the Detroit bench by Justin Abdelkader.

GAME THREE — *MAY 20, 2013*

Chicago 1 at Detroit 3

Detroit leads series 2–1

Allowing two goals in just 31 seconds is a bad sign if you hope to win a playoff game, and that's exactly what the Blackhawks did in the first period of Game 3. As a result, their 3–1 loss to Detroit left them trailing a series for the first time in the 2013 playoffs.

Despite peppering Red Wings goalie Jimmy Howard with 40 shots, the Presidents' Trophy winners were limited to one goal for the second straight game. It was just the third time in 2013 that the Blackhawks had lost consecutive games in regulation time.

"It takes something like this to slap you in the face, so to speak, to really understand what adversity is and how tough the playoffs can be," Chicago captain Jonathan Toews said. "A lot of guys in this room have been in tough positions before in the playoffs, and that's never stopped us. We know this is a long series and we're going to be fighting until the end."

With a spectacular individual effort, Gustav Nyquist gave the Red Wings a 1–0 lead at the 7:49 mark of the first period. The Swedish-born NHL rookie sped into the Chicago zone, cut left past Brent Seabrook, and outwaited both the sprawling defenseman and goalie before lifting a bad-angle shot into the net.

The Blackhawks were still wondering what had happened when Detroit went up 2–0 at 8:20. Defenseman Michal Rozsival turned the puck over in his own end,

Detroit's Henrik Zetterberg tries to move out front while Corey Crawford minds the Chicago goal.

Conference Semifinals – Chicago Blackhawks vs. Detroit Red Wings

43

Action is intense as players from both sides fight for the puck in front of Detroit goalie Jimmy Howard.

enabling Cory Emmerton to set up Patrick Eaves for two chances to Corey Crawford's right. The second one trickled past the Chicago goalie, and Drew Miller went hard to the net to shovel it over the goal line.

Meanwhile, Chicago coach Joel Quenneville wasn't happy with his team's inability to pressure Howard from close range.

"We've still got to find a way to get [to the net]," Quenneville said. "We've got to be willing to find a way to get to the net. You find a way through there, you get rewarded. It's not easy to penetrate, but you've got to be willing, and you've got to be committed to doing that. You've got to find a way."

Patrick Kane cut the deficit to 2–1 at 4:35 of the third period. His second goal of the series came on a breakaway set up by Duncan Keith, Kane hustling in to beat Howard through the five-hole.

The goal energized the visitors, and just over a minute later, the Blackhawks thought they had scored the equalizer on a Viktor Stalberg shot. The goal was waved off, however, because the referees ruled that Andrew Shaw interfered in the crease.

Backed by the fine goaltending of Jimmy Howard, Detroit won Game 3 to take a 2–1 series lead and gain control of the best-of-seven series.

Pavel Datsyuk nullified what looked like a potential Chicago comeback with a scintillating goal at 6:46 of the third. On the rush, the Russian superstar took a cross-ice pass from Johan Franzen and wired a wrister from the left faceoff circle past Crawford high on the stick side.

After dropping six straight games to Chicago in the regular season and losing the second-round opener, the Red Wings were now in the driver's seat. It was a remarkable turn of events for a team that for most of the regular season looked like it might miss the play-offs altogether.

Conference Semifinals – Chicago Blackhawks vs. Detroit Red Wings

45

GAME FOUR — *MAY 23, 2013*

Chicago 0 at Detroit 2

Detroit leads series 3–1

Detroit pushed Chicago to the brink of elimination with a shutout victory in Game 4, stunning any prognosticators who had forecast an easy series for the Blackhawks. Jakub Kindl's power-play goal midway through the second period proved to be the winner in front of an ecstatic Detroit crowd of 20,066.

It was the first time Chicago had lost three straight games all year, and the prognosis looked bleak for fans in the Windy City.

Detroit goalie Jimmy Howard was superb in recording his shutout of the 2013 postseason. While the game was scoreless in the first period, the 29-year-old native of Syracuse, N.Y., made 14 of his 28 saves on the night, many of them difficult.

It wasn't a night to remember for Chicago captain Jonathan Toews, though. The 2010 Conn Smythe Trophy winner was penalized three straight times for stick fouls in the middle period, and the frustrated center of Detroit's attention was sitting in the box when Kindl scored.

"Obviously I disagree with the calls, but it's in the heat of the moment," said Toews. "They see what they see. I've got to be careful of my stick. That doesn't help my team."

Commenting on Toews' rash of penalties, Detroit defenseman Jonathan Ericsson said, "We'd like to

Chicago captain Jonathan Toews is all business as he readies himself for a faceoff.

Detroit's Justin Abdelkader tries to deflect the puck in mid-air as goalie Corey Crawford looks on.

Conference Semifinals – Chicago Blackhawks vs. Detroit Red Wings

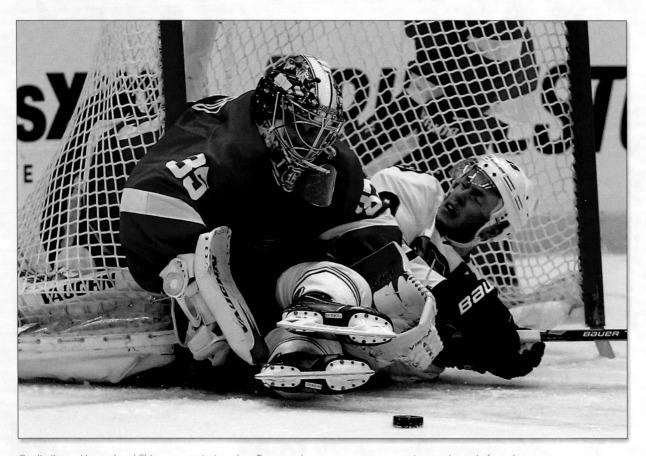

Goalie Jimmy Howard and Chicago captain Jonathan Toews make uneasy crease companions at the end of a rush.

keep him in the box. He's not as good for them in the box."

Kindl's blast through traffic, with Justin Abdelkader providing the screen in front, eluded Blackhawks goalie Corey Crawford at 10:03 of the second.

"Biggest goal of my life so far," the Czech-born rearguard said. "There's not a lot of time out there, so when I got it, I hesitated a half-second. When the defenseman went down to one knee, I went short side."

Could Detroit eliminate a Chicago team that started the 2012-13 season with a League-record 24 consecutive games without a regulation loss? The Blackhawks knew this was no time to dwell on history.

"There's no use hanging our heads," forward Patrick Sharp said. "Our backs are against the wall. We have to play our best game in Chicago. There's no other option. We can dig in here. We can find a way. . .for each other, for our team, for our city. We can find a way to get it done."

Dan Cleary's empty-net goal with 39 seconds remaining capped off Detroit's triumph. But the Red Wings hadn't booked their tickets to the Western Conference Final just yet. Goalie Jimmy Howard knew the Blackhawks would play with fire and fury to avoid elimination in Game 5.

"They're going to play even more desperate on Saturday night," said Howard. "We're going to have to match it. We can't rest on our laurels here. We played well the last three games, but we're going to have to ratchet it up even more Saturday night. The hardest win of the series is that fourth one. It's going to be another battle Saturday night."

Meanwhile, Toews, despite going goalless for the ninth straight playoff game, continued to sound the trumpet of optimism: "Eventually, something's got to give. We're too good a team. We've got too much talent. For as hard as we're working, something's got to go our way."

GAME FIVE — *MAY 25, 2013*

Detroit 1 at **Chicago 4**
Detroit leads series 3–2

Second-year NHLer Andrew Shaw is best-known as a tough competitor and relentless agitator. But the 2011 fifth-round pick of the Blackhawks also has a knack for timely goals, and he proved it in Chicago's must-win Game 5 at the "Madhouse on Madison."

Shaw scored twice, including the second-period game-winner, to lift Chicago to a 4–1 victory over Detroit, preserving the Blackhawks' bid for their second Stanley Cup in the last four years. Naturally, the 21-year-old shared the credit with his teammates.

"It was a great effort by everyone," Shaw said. "It's a team win. Everyone competed and everyone battled, and we played desperate hockey. That's what we need to do from here on out. We didn't want a great season like this to end like this. We came out hard in the first and created momentum through the game, and we just took off with it."

Bryan Bickell and Jonathan Toews — at long last — also scored for the Blackhawks, who dominated territorially, outshooting the Red Wings, 45–26.

Coach Joel Quenneville's decision to stack his top line with his three best players — Patrick Kane, Toews, and Patrick Sharp — paid dividends as the trio shone for the full 60 minutes. Likewise, reconvening the

Andrew Shaw celebrates one of his two goals in Chicago's crucial 4–1 win over Detroit in Game 5..

Conference Semifinals – Chicago Blackhawks vs. Detroit Red Wings

49

The Blackhawks celebrate their Game 5 victory.

Corey Crawford makes a great pad save off a quick shot from Gustav Nyquist.

longtime pairing of Duncan Keith and Brent Seabrook on the blue line also paid off. Their play was confident, and Keith garnered two assists.

Dan Cleary had the lone marker for Detroit, which missed a golden chance to advance to the Western Conference Final for the fourth time in the last eight years.

"We weren't good enough tonight at all as far as our plan or what we have to do to be successful," said Red Wings coach Mike Babcock. "There was too much space and [the Blackhawks] were freewheeling around and having fun. It just goes to show you how hard it is to win, and you've got to compete and do things right if you want to be successful."

Bickell got the party started at 14:08 for the United Center faithful, swiping home a rebound as Detroit goalie Jimmy Howard flopped in vain. But Cleary made it a 1–1 game at 9:37 of the second period after converting a rebound from Henrik Zetterberg's right-side shot on the rush.

Less than four minutes later, Chicago's power play came to life after failing to click on the previous 15 opportunities. Shaw deflected home Duncan Keith's point shot to give the Blackhawks a 2–1 lead.

"[Shaw] was taking a beating in front," said Sharp admiringly. "He probably got knocked down four or five times, and he still had energy left to celebrate after he scored."

Another man-advantage goal carried some important symbolic weight for Chicago. Toews, who hadn't scored yet in the playoffs, finally came through with a big one. Marian Hossa faked a shot and then fed it down low to the captain, whose rising shot went off Howard and under the crossbar to make it 3–1. Toews celebrated with unfettered jubilation – and relief.

Shaw's 4–1 goal came at 6:58 of the third. He corralled a Viktor Stalberg shot that went off the end boards, tucking it behind Howard, who had come out to challenge the play. The goal put the icing on the cake of what was an emphatic win and a clear message to the Red Wings.

Detroit got the game's last three power-play opportunities, but was unable to score on netminder Corey Crawford.

Conference Semifinals – Chicago Blackhawks vs. Detroit Red Wings

51

GAME SIX — *MAY 27, 2013*

Chicago 4 at Detroit 3

Series tied 3–3

It wasn't full of pretty goals, but Game 6 at Joe Louis Arena boasted plenty of passion as the Blackhawks fought for their playoff lives and the Red Wings were eager to close out the series. For the second straight game, however, the top-seeded Blackhawks came out victorious under the greatest of pressure. They forced a seventh and deciding game, thanks to three third-period goals in less than nine minutes.

"I think all our hard work is paying off," said Chicago captain Jonathan Toews. "We're finding ways, we're doing the right things to score goals and we're confident when we get those chances that they're going to go in somehow. We've got that momentum; we want to keep it."

Michael Frolik scored the eventual winner midway through the third. It came on a penalty shot that was awarded to him after he got hacked from behind on a breakaway by Detroit blueliner Carlo Colaiacovo. On his attempt, Frolik raced in on Jimmy Howard and lifted a backhander over the goalie's glove.

The Czech forward's success made him the first player in NHL history with two career penalty-shot goals in the playoffs. Frolik's other such goal came against Vancouver's Cory Schneider in a 4–3 overtime win in Game 6 of the 2011 Western Conference Quarterfinals.

While Howard had grabbed most of the goaltending-related headlines in this series, this was a night when Corey Crawford shone for Chicago, posting 35 saves and a .921 save percentage.

Marian Hossa staked Chicago to a 1–0 lead at 3:53, banging home a rebound in front. The net came off its

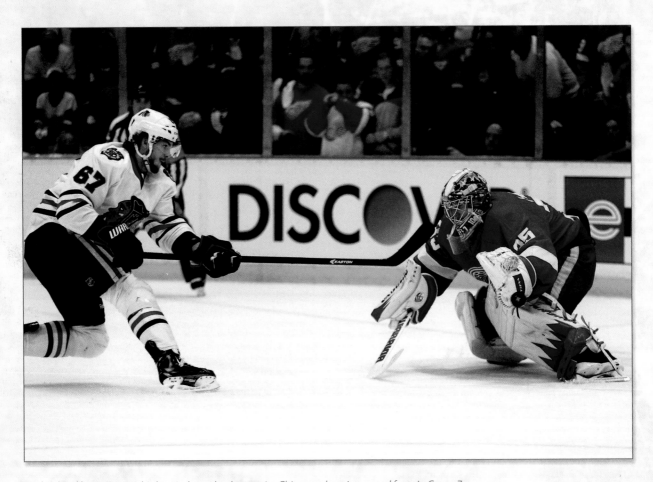

Michael Frolik scores on a third-period penalty shot to give Chicago a key victory and force in Game 7.

Goalie Corey Crawford makes the save as Detroit's Justin Abdelkader watches the puck roll past the Chicago goal.

Conference Semifinals – Chicago Blackhawks vs. Detroit Red Wings

53

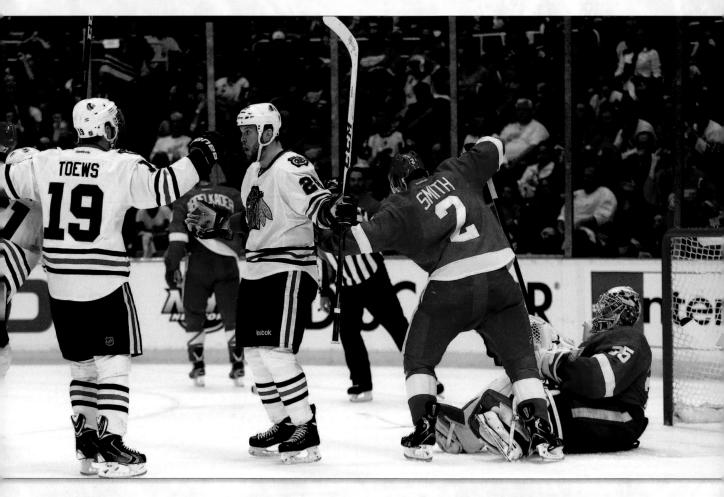

Bryan Bickell celebrates his third-period goal that gave Chicago a 3-2 lead.

moorings just an instant after the puck crossed the line, but video review revealed it was a good goal.

Detroit tied it up with 1:09 left in the first period, though, as Patrick Eaves converted the rebound from a Drew Miller shot.

Halfway through the second period, Detroit went up 2–1 on what might have been a very deflating goal against a team less resilient than Chicago. Joakim Andersson came down the left side and floated a shot that Crawford missed with his glove.

"It was a knuckle puck," said Andersson. "It's hard for the goalie to see those sometimes."

The Blackhawks refused to quit in the third period. Just 51 seconds in, Michal Handzus notched his first goal of the postseason, finishing off a Niklas Hjalmarsson centering pass from the corner to make it 2–2 and give Chicago renewed life.

Bryan Bickell stayed hot with his fifth playoff goal, outbattling Detroit's Brendan Smith in front of the net to put the rebound from a Jonathan Toews shot past Howard at 5:48 to give Chicago a stunning 3–2 lead.

After Frolik made it 4–2, all but silencing the Detroit crowd, the Red Wings kept fighting. Damien Brunner gave them one last gasp, hammering home a Pavel Datsyuk set-up from the top of the left faceoff circle with 52 seconds left. But that was as close as Detroit would get.

Red Wings coach Mike Babcock wasn't fessing up to any worries after allowing the opposition to take his squad to Game 7. "I love Game 7s," he enthused. "I'm excited about it. We've got a chance to push them out of the playoffs. Should be a lot of fun."

Of course, fun, like beauty, is in the eye of the beholder.

GAME SEVEN — MAY 29, 2013

Detroit 1 at **Chicago 2** (Seabrook 3:35 OT)
Chicago wins series 4–3

In a thrilling and sometimes controversial Game 7, it was fitting that overtime was required to settle this classic series. Chicago became the 25th club in NHL history to come back from a 3-1 deficit to win a best-of-seven series.

Brent Seabrook became the hero when he cut over the Detroit blue line into the middle of the ice and powered a slap shot that dinged off Niklas Kronwall's skate and high past the glove of goalie Jimmy Howard. Seabrook screamed with ecstasy, his face arched skyward, as his teammates mobbed him on the sideboards.

"I know Kronwall; he's a great defenseman," said Seabrook. "He tried to get out there and block it. I just wanted to get it past him and on net so I could change. Luckily, it went in."

Detroit's Dan Cleary summed up his team's emotions: "It is a good team we played. Guys should be proud and disappointed. We had a chance, three chances, to close them out, and we just didn't get it done."

Realistically, the Red Wings went deeper into the playoffs than almost anyone expected them to. After losing veteran stars such as Nicklas Lidstrom and Tomas Holmstrom to retirement and barely squeaking into the playoffs, the seventh-seeded club, captained by Henrik Zetterberg, gave the mighty Blackhawks all they could handle.

Patrick Sharp celebrates his second-period goal that gave the Blackhawks a 1–0 lead.

Conference Semifinals – Chicago Blackhawks vs. Detroit Red Wings

55

Brent Seabrook screams to the heavens after winning the series for Chicago with an overtime goal in Game 7.

The first period was scoreless, and was most notable for Valtteri Filppula's departure with a high ankle sprain after a mix-up with Chicago's Andrew Shaw.

Just 1:08 into the second period, however, Patrick Sharp's seventh playoff goal gave Chicago a 1–0 lead. He finished off a beautiful passing play on a three-on-one rush with Michal Handzus and Marian Hossa, which resulted from a sloppy Detroit line change.

"A couple of nice passes. I had an open net," said Sharp succinctly. "It was a big goal for us."

Continuing a pattern of clutch play in 2013, Zetterberg got the equalizer for Detroit 26 seconds into the third period. Gustav Nyquist gave him a lovely cross-ice pass and Zetterberg put it into the gaping net, as Crawford had overcommitted to Nyquist.

When all was said and done, the Blackhawks skated off victors after Game 7, escaping from a series deficit to advance to the Western Conference Final.

The United Center crowd went bananas when Chicago rearguard Niklas Hjalmarsson appeared to have scored the go-ahead goal with 1:49 remaining in the third period, pounding a sweet set-up by Andrew Shaw high inside Howard's left post. But the goal was called back because coincidental roughing minors had just been called on Detroit's Kyle Quincey and Chicago's Brandon Saad. Fortunately for the Blackhawks, Seabrook's overtime tally made that little dust-up moot.

Since Detroit will play in the Eastern Conference next season, these two clubs won't meet again in the playoffs – unless it's in the Stanley Cup Final. But this was a superb way to close out their Western Conference rivalry.

"Detroit played a great series," said Seabrook graciously. "We really had to find ourselves after the fourth game being down 3–1. I thought the boys responded well. We played a very good Game 5. I thought we played a very good Game 6. I thought we played very well tonight. Detroit gave us all they had. It was just nice to come out on the winning end of this."

Conference Semifinals – Chicago Blackhawks vs. Detroit Red Wings

57

GAME ONE — JUNE 1, 2013

Los Angeles 1 at **Chicago 2**

Chicago leads series 1–0

To dethrone the defending Stanley Cup champions, the Blackhawks would have to figure out a way to score on the NHL's hottest goalie. Putting two pucks past Jonathan Quick of the Los Angeles Kings in the second period of Game 1 proved to be sufficient – barely.

Quick, the 2012 Conn Smythe Trophy winner, came into the Western Conference Final with NHL-leading numbers: a 1.50 goals-against average, 948 save percentage and three shutouts. Early on in this first game, it looked like the American puckstopper might stymie the Blackhawks all by himself.

"[Quick is] one of the fastest goalies in the League, if not the fastest," said Chicago's Marian Hossa, who scored the eventual game-winner. "Whatever he sees, he's going to stop. You have to have traffic in front of him, pin him in the blue paint and put lots of pucks in the corners or in his feet and go for the second chances."

Like Chicago, fifth-seeded Los Angeles was coming off a grueling seven-game series, having defeated San Jose 2–1 in the clincher on a pair of Justin Williams goals.

The Presidents' Trophy winners outshot the Kings 17–2 in the first period, but Williams got the lone goal of the frame to put Los Angeles ahead. Dave Bolland whiffed on an attempt to clear the puck out of Chicago's zone, and Williams opportunistically swept the puck past Corey Crawford at 14:23.

The Blackhawks started forechecking better and going to the net more in the second period, and their efforts paid off. Patrick Sharp hustled into the Los Angeles zone and left a drop pass for Johnny Oduya. Quick stopped Oduya's shot with his left pad, but Sharp was right there to bang in the rebound at 12:29.

"That first shot against [Quick] is tough," said Blackhawks coach Joel Quenneville. "I think the

Chicago goalie Corey Crawford takes a breather during a stoppage in play.

Patrick Kane has a good scoring chance from in close, but can't beat Jonathan Quick.

volume of shots and traffic is the only way to get to this guy."

Hossa's winning goal proved the validity of Quenneville's theory. The Slovak power forward escaped Mike Richards' checking and got a stick on a drive by Duncan Keith, tipping it past Quick for a 2–1 lead at 16:22.

Keeping the Kings' top offensive players off the board, from Anze Kopitar to Drew Doughty, was another key to the Blackhawks' victory. Some of the Kings' top players – like captain Dustin Brown, who had a torn knee ligament – were playing injured, which didn't help their chances.

Outshot 36–22 on the night, the Kings admitted they had been outplayed. "We didn't deserve to win that game," said forward Jarret Stoll, who was back in the lineup after missing six games with a concussion. "That's the bottom line. I don't think any of us in here can say we deserved to win that game, and we didn't."

Chicago remained undefeated when leading after two periods in the playoffs (6–0). Meanwhile, Los Angeles lost for the sixth time in the postseason – oddly, by the same 2–1 score each time.

Now the question was whether Chicago would continue to carry the series with its speed and finesse or whether Los Angeles would rally by turning it into a grind-it-out matchup.

Conference Final – Chicago Blackhawks vs. Los Angeles Kings

59

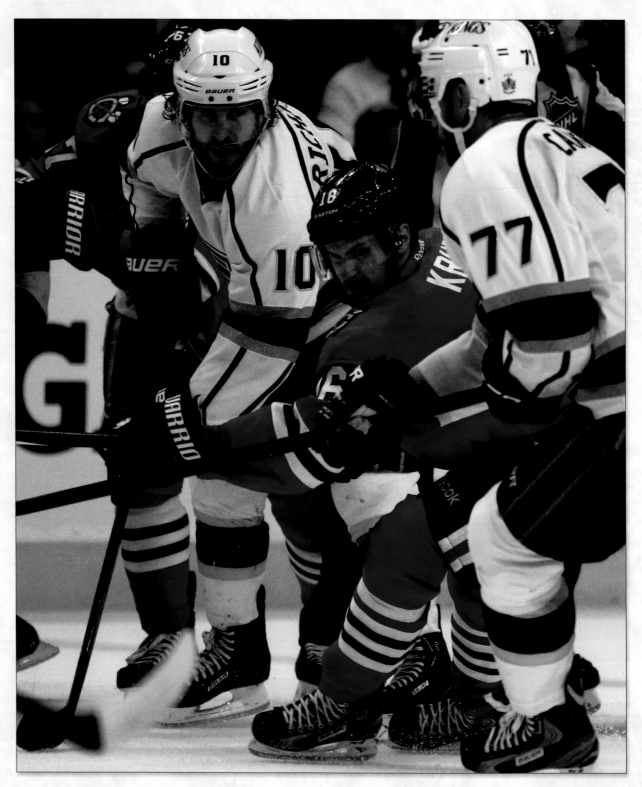

Chicago's Marcus Kruger fights for position near the Los Angeles goal against Mike Richards and Jeff Carter.

60

Conference Final – Chicago Blackhawks vs. Los Angeles Kings

GAME TWO — JUNE 2, 2013

Los Angeles 2 at **Chicago 4**
Chicago leads series 2–0

Building a 4–0 lead in a crucial Game 2 situation is never a bad thing. Chasing superstar goalie Jonathan Quick out of a game is arguably even better. Chicago achieved both of those feats in a surprisingly one-sided victory at United Center to go up 2–0 in the Western Conference Final. Patrick Sharp and Brandon Saad both had a pair of assists.

"We just haven't been finding a way," said Quick. "We have to find a way. [The Blackhawks] did their job. Now we have to go home and do our job."

Unusually, Quick seemed to be off his game this Sunday evening. It took just 1:54 for Andrew Shaw to open the scoring, taking a feed from Viktor Stalberg and beating Los Angeles. netminder cleanly with a shot off the inside of the left post.

Goals in the last minute of a period can often be backbreakers, and the game's outcome was clarified for the Kings when Brent Seabrook took a drop pass from Marian Hossa and powered home a slapper past Quick's blocker from the right faceoff circle, making it 2–0 at 19:09.

"Whoever is shooting the puck, we feel as a team that we have the confidence that it's going to go in at some point," said Chicago captain Jonathan Toews. "So we'll keep shooting the puck, creating those chances and trying to take [Quick's] confidence away."

The Blackhawks generated some good luck on their third goal, which came on the power play at 7:11 of the second period. Standing in front of the net, Bryan Bickell tucked the puck between his legs, collecting the rebound from Patrick Sharp's point shot from the middle of the ice. Kings defenseman Robyn Regehr inadvertently helped the puck into his own net.

Andrew Shaw's goal 1:54 into Game 2 set the tone for an impressive Chicago win, its second in two nights.

Conference Final – Chicago Blackhawks vs. Los Angeles Kings

61

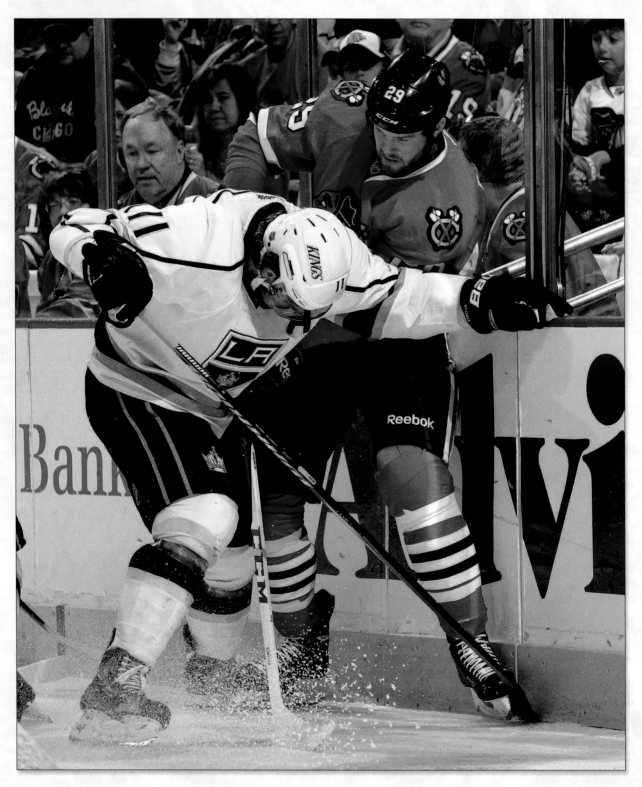

Bryan Bickell ties up Anze Kopitar behind the Chicago net.

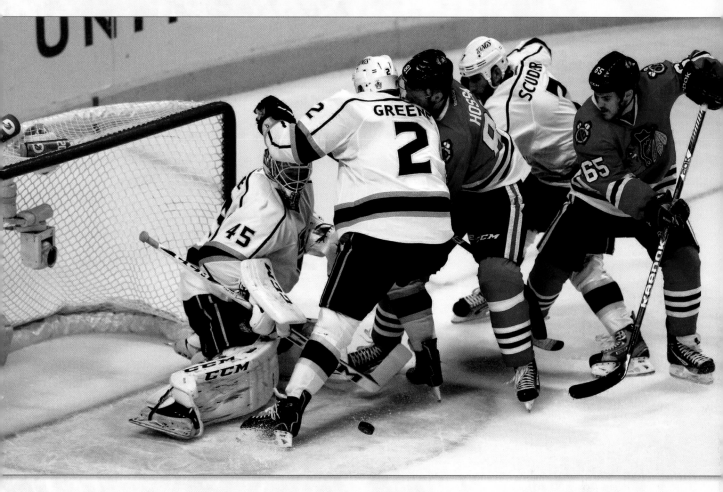

Almost, but not quite. Chicago presses for a goal, but Los Angeles clears the traffic in front for goalie Jonathan Bernier.

Just over two minutes later, Michal Handzus put the game out of reach with Chicago's fourth goal. Rushing in on a two-on-one break, the veteran Slovak took a pass from Sharp and, keeping his head up, scored with a quick release that beat Quick on the stick side.

Kings coach Darryl Sutter decided he had seen enough and pulled Quick, replacing him with backup Jonathan Bernier. It was the first time in 35 playoff games that the 27-year-old Connecticut native had allowed more than three goals, dating to a 4–3 overtime loss to the San Jose Sharks on April 25, 2011.

Despite the tough circumstances, Kings rookie Tyler Toffoli made his presence felt in his series debut. The 21-year-old assisted on Jeff Carter's goal from the left faceoff circle that spoiled Corey Crawford's shutout bid with 1:03 left in the second period.

Toffoli was playing in lieu of Mike Richards, who didn't suit up due to an upper-body injury after a hit he took from Dave Bolland late in the series opener. Toffoli added a power-play goal late in the game, whacking home a loose puck at the side of the net with 1:02 left in the third, but the Kings couldn't stage a late comeback.

Now Chicago would aim to beat the Kings in Los Angeles, a much more difficult proposition than winning at home before its own fans. The Kings were undefeated in 14 straight home games, dating to the end of the 2012–13 regular season. And they had already rallied from a 2–0 series deficit in these playoffs, storming back with four straight victories to oust St. Louis in the first round.

"It seems like we have a lot of momentum," said Patrick Kane. "We'll try to keep that. Game 3 is a big game. It's a huge game."

GAME THREE — *JUNE 4, 2013*

Chicago 1 at Los Angeles 3

Chicago leads series 2–1

The Stanley Cup champions weren't going to go down without a fight. Buoyed by a two-point performance from defenseman Slava Voynov, including the winning goal, Los Angeles battled its way back into the series with a home-ice win in Game 3.

"We knew exactly the kind of game they were going to play and that they were going to have more confidence, more energy in their own building," said Chicago's Jonathan Toews. "We just didn't bring that same effort and that same pace. We know we have to be better than that in the next one."

It was a grittier and more focused outing from coach Darryl Sutter's crew on home ice as the Kings improved to 8–0 at STAPLES Center during the playoffs. And they won by again overcoming the absence of Mike Richards, who missed his second straight game.

Justin Williams opened the scoring for Los Angeles at 3:21, accepting a hard pass from Voynov in the left faceoff circle and beating Chicago's Corey Crawford on the stick side.

"We were just quicker. We were quicker everywhere on the ice," said Williams. "They're a transition team. They're an explosive offensive team if you give them opportunities. We limited their time and space because we were on our toes instead of our heels."

Los Angeles forward Justin Williams is stopped by Corey Crawford from the side of the Chicago goal.

Goalie Corey Crawford is supported by four teammates as the Kings storm the Blackhawks' goal.

Drew Doughty nearly gave Los Angeles a two-goal lead in the final minute of the first period, pounding a slap shot off the goal post. Voynov was more fortunate, scoring the 2–0 goal on a weird play at 6:37 of the second.

Rookie Tyler Toffoli found the Russian blueliner out front with a smart backhand feed through traffic from behind the goal line. Voynov leaned into a slap shot, but his stick broke and the puck fluttered into the net past a surprised Crawford.

The goal continued a history-making run for the 23-year-old from Chelyabinsk. It was Voynov's fifth of the playoffs, the most ever in one postseason for a Kings defenseman. It was his fourth game-winner, too, which set a club record for all skaters.

The never-say-die Blackhawks got on the board with just 34 seconds left in the middle frame. Big Bryan Bickell grabbed the puck behind the net and skated out front unchecked to complete a wraparound.

Conference Final – Chicago Blackhawks vs. Los Angeles Kings

65

The Blackhawks come close to scoring but are foiled by Jonathan Quick.

However, Los Angeles goalie Jonathan Quick was perfect the rest of the way. Stopping 19 of 20 shots on the evening, he stood his ground when the Blackhawks stormed his crease, including a fabulous close-range blocker save on Bickell with just over three minutes remaining in regulation.

"In your head, you tell yourself you got to play better in Game 4," Quick said. "I didn't like the goal I gave up, and there are some things I like to clean up for the next game. I just think from a team standpoint, it's good to win. You're down 2–0, you need a win."

Dwight King finished things off with an empty-netter at 19:32.

The Kings were back in business now, and the momentum seemed to have shifted. Heading into a pivotal Game 4, Chicago needed to respond appropriately and reassert its control of the series.

66

Conference Final – Chicago Blackhawks vs. Los Angeles Kings

GAME FOUR — *JUNE 6, 2013*

Chicago 3 at Los Angeles 2

Chicago leads series 3–1

Scoring early is always a plus, and although the Blackhawks were forced to battle back after quick Los Angeles goals in the first and second periods, Marian Hossa's tally 1:10 into the third proved to be the game-winner. Chicago took a stranglehold on this series by winning on the road and now had the opportunity to finish off the Kings in Game 5 in Chicago.

The Blackhawks didn't have Duncan Keith in the lineup because the former Norris Trophy winner was serving a one-game suspension for his high stick on Jeff Carter in the previous game.

That said, Chicago got tremendous performances from other blueliners who took advantage of their increased ice time. Playing 24:57, Niklas Hjalmarsson, for instance, chipped in a pair of assists, while Brent Seabrook logged a team-leading 26:20 of ice time.

From top to bottom, it was a resilient effort by the Blackhawks.

"We talked about it all season, especially in the playoffs, but our team game, our team 'D,' is really what's been doing such a great job," said Seabrook. "[Corey Crawford] in the net has been making some big saves. When the forwards are coming back like they are, it's making it easy for us. We're just trying to get back there quick and get outlet passes for our forwards to play with the puck."

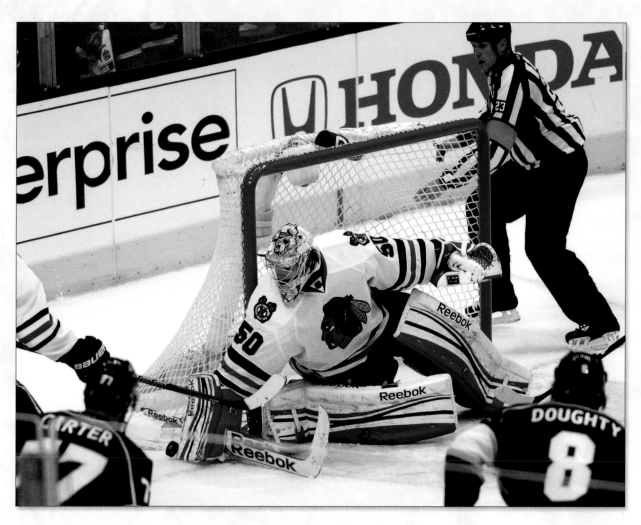

Corey Crawford makes a final save in the dying seconds as the Kings press, unsuccessfully, to tie the game.

Conference Final – Chicago Blackhawks vs. Los Angeles Kings

67

Game 4 didn't start out well for Chicago. Los Angeles netminder Jonathan Quick foiled Jonathan Toews on a glorious early breakaway chance. Slava Voynov then electrified the Kings faithful when his point shot from the middle of the ice beat Crawford at 3:28 for a 1–0 lead.

But Bryan Bickell maintained his torrid pace with the tying goal, his eighth of the postseason. He waltzed in over the Los Angeles blue line and flung a wrister on goal, which Quick surprisingly bobbled, allowing the puck to trickle in. Kings coach Darryl Sutter admitted afterward it was a "bad goal."

Dustin Penner restored the Kings' lead at 2:12 of the second period, charging to the net and pushing a centering pass from Carter through Quick's pads.

Patrick Kane had an answer for Chicago as this seesaw battle continued. When Bickell tipped a Hjalmarsson blast from the blue line that was

Brent Seabrook is upended by Dustin Penner of the Kings while teammate Niklas Hjalmarsson manages to get under the collision.

68

Conference Final – Chicago Blackhawks vs. Los Angeles Kings

Marian Hossa scores early in the third period to give Chicago a 3–2 win in Los Angeles and control of the series.

dribbling past Quick, Kane just nudged it over the goal line and made it 2–2 with 1:39 left in the middle frame.

Hossa's winning goal early in the third period was a beauty. He zoomed in on a two-on-one rush with Michal Handzus and one-timed the cross-ice feed from his Slovak comrade high past Quick, who had no chance. It was Chicago's first lead of the night, and it wouldn't be surrendered.

Neither team could capitalize on power plays later in the third. The biggest kill of the night came when Michael Frolik was sent off for high-sticking at 15:23. The Blackhawks didn't let the Kings get a single shot on goal at a time when they were desperate for a goal to stay in the series.

Crawford outduelled Quick between the pipes as Chicago outshot Los Angeles, 28–21. The Montreal-born netminder also summed up what he and his teammates were feeling about returning to United Center with a 3–1 series lead: "It's going to be exciting to have a chance to move on in our building."

Conference Final – Chicago Blackhawks vs. Los Angeles Kings

69

GAME FIVE — *JUNE 8, 2013*

Los Angeles 3 at **Chicago 4** (Kane 31:40 OT)

Chicago wins series 4–1

Pure magic. That might be the best way to describe the game that sent Chicago to the Stanley Cup Final for the 12th time in franchise history and second time in four years. Patrick Kane scored a hat trick to propel the Blackhawks past the Kings, and his double-overtime winner set up by Jonathan Toews was absolutely spectacular.

"Right now, I think it's almost like I'm in a different zone, like in the Twilight Zone or something," Kane gushed. "I'm kind of out of it. It's definitely a good feeling, though."

With the Boston Bruins having won the Eastern Conference, the victory set up the first clash of Original Six teams in the Stanley Cup Final since the Montreal Canadiens vanquished the New York Rangers in 1979.

Chicago squandered a 2–0 lead and allowed the Kings to tie the game with less than 10 seconds left in the third period. Coming out on top despite those lapses was a testament to the club's intestinal fortitude.

The Kings were disconsolate about being dethroned as Stanley Cup champions. "You play hockey in June to win," Justin Williams said. "You get this far, to not have a chance to defend it, it's frustrating. I can't stand looking at somebody else raise that Cup, and now we're going to have to do it."

Duncan Keith returned to the lineup after serving a one-game suspension and had an immediate impact. His 1–0 goal at 3:42 showed that Kings goalie Jonathan Quick wasn't at his very best. Keith charged down the left side, crossed the blue line and powered a slap shot between the pads of a kneeling Quick.

Just before the six-minute mark, Kane notched the 2–0 goal, picking up a Toews rebound and patiently waiting for Quick and Los Angeles' defenders to sprawl before whipping it high into the net.

Kane, who scored the Stanley Cup winner in over-time of Game 6 against Philadelphia in 2010, had

Marian Hossa is stopped point-blank by Los Angeles goalie Jonathan Quick.

Patrick Kane scores his second goal of the game to give the Blackhawks a 3–2 lead.

been criticized for not producing enough since then – just four goals in 28 playoff games prior to Game 6. But he silenced naysayers with this virtuoso outing.

Things improved for the Kings in the middle frame. Dwight King made it 2–1 at 9:28 with a shorthanded goal, shoveling a loose puck through Corey Crawford. Two minutes later, Quick stoned a determined Marian Hossa on a partial breakaway to lift team spirits.

At 3:34 of the third, Anze Kopitar scored his first goal in six games to pull Los Angeles even. Kane then made it 3–2 with 3:52 left, causing most fans at the jubilant United Center to believe their hometown squad had already won.

Not so fast.

In his return to the lineup, Mike Richards came up huge for Los Angeles, deflecting home Kopitar's shot from the sideboards with just 9.4 seconds left to tie it up. The crowd was stunned. Could the Blackhawks recover?

Absolutely. But the climax would have to wait until the second overtime. On a two-on-one rush that will remain legendary in Chicago, Toews skimmed a cross-ice pass to Kane and he one-timed it high past Quick at 11:40. Kane flung himself to his knees in wild celebration. The Blackhawks were bound for the Final against Boston.

"The tradition of the Bruins and the Blackhawks is special," Chicago coach Joel Quenneville said. "The rivalry could return instantly come Game 1. It's good for hockey."

Conference Final – Chicago Blackhawks vs. Los Angeles Kings

71

Teammates mob Patrick Kane after his overtime goal advanced the Blackhawks to their second Stanley Cup Final in four years.

GAME ONE — *JUNE 12, 2013*

Boston 3 at **Chicago 4** (Shaw 52:08 OT)
Chicago leads series 1–0

The best-of-seven Stanley Cup Final became a best-of-eight after Game 1 took nearly six periods of play to determine a winner. Yet, incredibly, Chicago rallied from two goals down in the third, staved off two penalties for too many men in overtime and got a fluky goal midway through the sixth period from Andrew Shaw to take a 1–0 series lead.

"We've preached it – go to the net, you'll find a way to get a greasy goal," Shaw said of Michal Roszival's shot that bounced first off Dave Bolland and then himself before sneaking past Boston goalie Tuukka Rask. "We did a heck of a job of it there in the third overtime."

The Bruins played a perfect road game for 50 minutes and must have felt a little down by the end of a long game. They scored the only goal of the first period, taking a 1–0 lead at 13:11 and silencing the often raucous United Center crowd. David Krejci

chased a loose puck deep into the Blackhawks' end and bounced off a check from Niklas Hjalmarsson. Krejci then got the puck to Nathan Horton at the side of the net, and Horton in turn found Milan Lucic, who fired a quick shot over the glove of Corey Crawford.

The Blackhawks had come out like gangbusters, hitting everything in sight and having the better of puck possession, but they managed few shots on Tuukka Rask in the Bruins' goal. Lucic's goal turned the tide, though, and Boston seemed poised and in control the rest of the opening 20 minutes.

Lucic made it a 2–0 game in the first minute of the second thanks to a turnover at center ice. And again it was Krejci who made the set-up, dropping the puck to Lucic in the high slot for a perfect shot just 51 seconds after the start of the period.

The Blackhawks made a game of it just two minutes later on a goal similar to Lucic's first one. This time it was Marian Hossa who beat Horton to the puck, which came out to Brandon Saad in the slot. He ripped a quick shot over Rask's shoulder at 3:08 to cut the lead in half and get Chicago emotionally into the

The crease of Boston goalie Tuukka Rask is crowded as players from both sides jostle for position.

Stanley Cup Final – Chicago Blackhawks vs. Boston Bruins

73

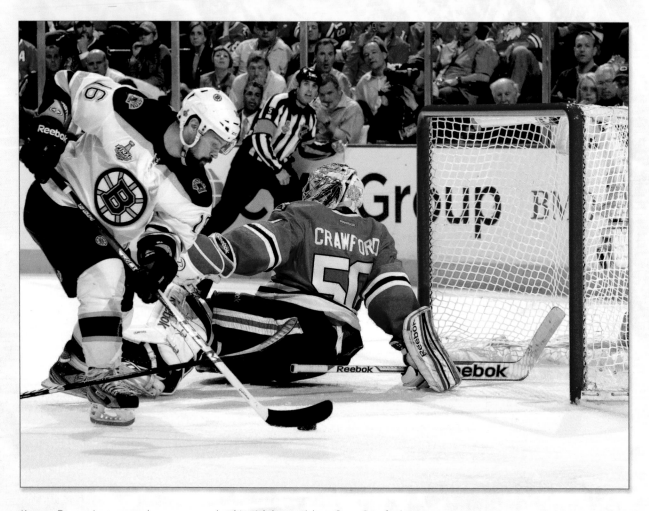

Kaspars Daugavins seems to have a sure goal on his stick, but can't beat Corey Crawford in overtime.

game for the first time since the opening few shifts.

The Blackhawks had the only three power plays in the period, including a five-on-three for more than a minute, but the Bruins' penalty killers were sensational and allowed not a single shot. The period ended as it began, with the visitors in front by a goal.

The Bruins got their first power play of the game early in the third when Michael Frolik took a tripping penalty 200 feet from his own goal, and they didn't waste any time converting. Patrice Bergeron ripped a shot past Crawford just 18 seconds after the penalty to silence the crowd once again.

But as was the case in the second, the Blackhawks struck back quickly. Less than two minutes later, Shaw got a loose puck off a turnover at the Boston blue line and set up Bolland for a perfect one-timer in front.

Just like that it was 3–2 and the Blackhawks had some momentum again.

This time they gained more and more confidence and ended up tying the game on a lucky bounce. Johnny Oduya's point shot banked off the skate of defenseman Andrew Ference and past Rask to make it 3–3 with less than eight minutes left in regulation.

That set the stage for a remarkable overtime, a lucky bounce and a lead the Blackhawks felt fortunate to have.

"You can dwell on it as much as you want, but at the end of the day you've got to be able to turn the page and focus on Game 2," Lucic said. "Shoulda, woulda, coulda is not going to get you anywhere. It's not going to win us a game in the end. And I think we need to focus on Game 2 as fast as we can."

74

Stanley Cup Final – Chicago Blackhawks vs. Boston Bruins

Dave Bolland converts Andrew Shaw's pass to cut Boston's lead in half in the third period.

Stanley Cup Final – Chicago Blackhawks vs. Boston Bruins

75

GAME TWO — *JUNE 15, 2013*
Boston 2 at Chicago 1 (Paille 13:48 OT)
Series tied 1–1

While the Blackhawks could have felt a bit fortunate to have won the series opener, they felt more than a little disappointed to have lost Game 2. But the loss was due largely to the great play of Boston goalie Tuukka Rask, who held the fort nobly while Chicago did everything but run up the score in a lopsided first period.

Rask allowed only one goal through 20 minutes despite the Bruins being outshot 19-4 in the opening period. Boston coach Claude Julien rallied his trips during the intermission, and the Bruins responded, controlling the play the rest of the way, especially in overtime. "It looked like they had more guys out there than we did," Rask noted of the strong Chicago start. "They were pouncing on every single puck in front of net and had a lot of chances. We definitely played pretty bad. But, you know, it was good that we were only down by one, and we regrouped after that."

Chicago opened the scoring at 11:22 on a Patrick Sharp goal, an inevitable tally given how dominant the Blackhawks had been. And they felt they went up 2–0 a minute later when Marian Hossa pushed the puck over the goal line, but the goal went to video review and it was determined that referee Wes McAuley had blown the play dead before the puck entered the net.

Chicago's Michal Handzus and Boston's Johnny Boychuk mix it up in front of the Boston goal.

Eight players crowd Tuukka Rask, who makes the save despite intense pressure from the Blackhawks.

Perhaps the Blackhawks were as disheartened by the results of the first period as the Bruins were buoyed, but whatever the case Boston slowly turned the tide in the second and gathered momentum. They tied the game at 5:02 thanks to some quick work around the Chicago goal. Daniel Paille tried a wrap-around, and although Corey Crawford made the save the puck slid free to Chris Kelly, who snapped it home.

The longer the game went, the more the Bruins were in control. The Blackhawks stopped going hard to the Boston goal and didn't generate many chances in the third, and in the overtime they played hesitatingly while the Bruins played with confidence. Boston had the best chances of the fourth period and

was rewarded when Brent Seabrook tried to clear the puck along the boards.

Adam McQuaid kept the puck in at the blue line and passed to Tyler Seguin, who fired a cross-ice pass to a wide-open Paille, whose quick shot went past Crawford's extended glove, off the post and in. In the blink of an eye, the series was tied and the Bruins had claimed home-ice advantage.

"We just didn't continue to play the way we'd been playing," admitted Chicago captain Jonathan Toews. "We let them have the puck a little too often. We didn't move our feet. We were too easy to check."

Boston outshot Chicago 24–14 after the first period and headed home with the psychological advantage.

Stanley Cup Final – Chicago Blackhawks vs. Boston Bruins

77

Patrick Sharp celebrates his first-period goal with teammates, but their happiness was short-lived as the Bruins rallied for a road win.

78

Stanley Cup Final – Chicago Blackhawks vs. Boston Bruins

GAME THREE — *JUNE 17, 2013*

Chicago 0 at **Boston 2**
Boston leads series 2–1

The Bruins carried their momentum from Chicago to Boston, from overtime in Game 2 to the start of Game 3, overwhelming Chicago in a convincing 2–0 victory to take control of the series. Tuukka Rask recorded his third shutout of the playoffs, but didn't have to make too many great saves due to a strong defensive effort in front of him. Chicago lacked the energy needed to fight through checks, go hard to the net and create "dirty" scoring chances, which are necessary to win games in the playoffs.

"I thought we did a lot of good things tonight," said Chicago defenseman Duncan Keith. "I thought we had a lot of the play and pushed the pace, just for whatever reason we can't capitalize on a chance. But time's running out. We've got to get a goal. I think we just have to come up with a big game and find a way to win."

The game started off on a bad note for the Blackhawks even before the drop of the puck. Marian Hossa, who skated in warmups, was a late scratch, and coach Joel Quenneville was forced to insert Ben Smith into the lineup. The loss of one of Chicago's top offensive threats helped Boston, of course.

The first period offered positives for both teams, although the Bruins were the more impressive squad. For the visiting Blackhawks, they responded well after their Game 2 loss and came out hard, taking the crowd out of the game for the most part and having the better of the puck possession.

However, while they moved easily into the Boston end, they were unable to get into the slot and scoring areas, and most of their shots on Rask were harmless and from long range.

Like all of his teammates, Andrew Shaw couldn't get the puck past Tuukka Rask in Game 3.

Stanley Cup Final – Chicago Blackhawks vs. Boston Bruins

79

The Blackhawks were a frustrated group after being outplayed and outhustled by the Bruins in Game 3.

The Bruins, on the other hand, had the puck less but had the better scoring chances, notably a short-handed breakaway by Brad Marchand set up by a beautiful pass from Zdeno Chara. Marchand, however, lost control of the puck and failed to get a shot.

The period ended in a scoreless tie, but the Bruins came out to start the second in impressive fashion, opening the scoring thanks to Daniel Paille, the over-time hero in Game 2.

The Blackhawks were unable to clear the puck around the boards, and Paille deftly stripped Dave Bolland and let go a quick snap shot in one motion, beating Corey Crawford at 2:13. The Bruins followed the opening goal with wave after wave of confident play and might have increased their lead if not for Crawford's calm in the blue paint.

Finally, the Bruins did, indeed, make it 2–0 thanks to two man advantages. The penalties overlapped by 11 seconds, and as the Blackhawks got one man back, Jaromir Jagr made a nifty cross-crease pass to Patrice Bergeron at 14:05.

"It was a great pass," Bergeron noted. "I was expecting the puck to come, but it was a perfect play. I had to kind of settle it down a bit. I just had to put it in, and, thankfully, I did that."

Although there was plenty of time left, the game was pretty much out of reach due to Boston's strong defensive efforts. The Blackhawks played desperate hockey in the third, but it was more of the same – the Bruins were the more tenacious team and collapsed around Rask with great success. It had now been more than 122 minutes since the Blackhawks last scored.

80

Stanley Cup Final – Chicago Blackhawks vs. Boston Bruins

Blackhawks captain Jonathan Toews was neutralized by Patrice Bergeron and the Bruins throughout Game 3.

Stanley Cup Final – Chicago Blackhawks vs. Boston Bruins

81

GAME FOUR — *JUNE 19, 2013*

Chicago 6 at Boston 5 (Seabrook 9:51 OT)

Series tied 2–2

No one said it was going to be easy, and no one said it was going to be a short series. Just as they split the first two games in Chicago, so, too, did the Blackhawks and Bruins split a pair in Boston thanks to Brent Seabrook's overtime goal in one of the wildest Stanley Cup Final games in recent memory. Both teams could have won – and both teams could have lost. But on this night, it was the Blackhawks that went home with the victory.

From Boston's perspective, the team came back three times to force overtime. From Chicago's, the team went on the attack in a way it had failed to do for the first three games. And, for the first time, both teams would admit their goaltending left a little something to be desired.

"It was time to put all those other games behind us, the games where we struggled to score, forget about it, just find a way to do what you do," said Chicago captain Jonathan Toews. "It was fun to see the puck go in as often as it did tonight. We know we can be better defensively. But we'll use that confidence and try our best to pounce on them in Game 5."

The Blackhawks held leads of 1–0, 3–1, 4–2, and 5–4, but for every goal they scored the Bruins seemed to have a response. The visitors got the early lead while short-handed. With Johnny Oduya in the box, Brandon Saad and Michal Handzus broke in on a two-on-two, with Handzus fighting off a check from Patrice Bergeron and knocking in a great pass from Saad to make it 1–0.

Brent Seabrook beats Tuukka Rask for the overtime winner as Jonathan Toews and Zdeno Chara look on.

82

Stanley Cup Final – Chicago Blackhawks vs. Boston Bruins

Marcus Kruger picks up his own rebound and lifts the puck over Tuukka Rask to make it a 4–2 game for the Blackhawks.

But Saad twice failed to clear the puck on a later Boston power play, and Rich Peverley tied the game with a shot that surprised Corey Crawford. The Blackhawks continued to press early in the second period and were rewarded twice.

Jonathan Toews ended a 10-game scoring drought by tipping in a Michal Rozsival shot at 6:33 and then newly-reunited linemate Patrick Kane made it 3–1 two minutes later when he backhanded a shot into the empty side of the net.

Normally a 3–1 lead might produce conservative play, but on this night the Bruins pushed the play as the fought back to tie the game. They cut the lead in half when Milan Lucic deposited a rebound from a Zdeno Chara point shot, but the Blackhawks quickly responded to make it 4-2.

Defenseman Dennis Seidenberg made an unwise pinch at the Chicago blue line to create an odd-man rush, and while Rask made a great save on Marcus Kruger's first shot, the Blackhawks' forward got his own rebound and lifted it into the net with Rask on his stomach.

By this point it was clear that no lead was safe. Indeed, Bergeron scored late in the second and early in the third to tie the game, once again giving Boston fans hope that their team could take a formidable 3-1 series lead.

Midway through the third Patrick Sharp scored on a power play, the Blackhawks' first man-advantage goal of the series and his League-leading 10th of the postseason. Sharp had been stopped twice on break-aways earlier, but his go-ahead goal lasted less than a minute. Johnny Boychuk's slap shot eluded Crawford over the glove, the fourth of five goals to do so, and the game was now tied 5–5.

The Bruins had the better of the chances in the final minutes, but the game was up for grabs once it went to overtime. Seabrook's winner was a quick slapshot that Rask didn't see because of a big-time battle in front between Chara and Toews, both of whom were fighting for position as they had almost every shift, all series.

"It's exciting," Seabrook said. "Everybody worked so hard tonight, everybody's worked so hard throughout the playoffs. We're all contributing. It doesn't matter if I score, or anybody else scores; it's nice to get the win and move on to the next day. I think it's definitely exciting to score in an overtime game, an overtime goal. But at the end of the day it's just a win and we still need two more."

The Boston philosophy was much the same as the series entered its final phase. "You've got to bring your best," said Bergeron. "It is time to focus on Game 5 now. There is nothing you can do about the previous four. We're even, and it is about the best-of-three now. You have to look at it that way, and go out and be ready for Game 5."

Like reunited linemate Jonathan Toews, Patrick Kane scored in Game 4 on this pretty backhander.

84

Stanley Cup Final – Chicago Blackhawks vs. Boston Bruins

GAME FIVE — *JUNE 22, 2013*
Boston 1 at Chicago 3
Chicago leads series 3–2

This is why teams battle throughout the regular season – to get home-ice advantage in the playoffs. And now, when it counted the most, the Blackhawks used that advantage to skate to a vital 3–1 victory in Game 5, giving themselves two opportunities to win the Stanley Cup.

Patrick Kane led the way on offense with two goals, while Corey Crawford was sharp in the back end, atoning for his play three nights earlier when he allowed five goals. In addition to the goals and scoreboard, the game offered other drama as Jonathan Toews, who assisted on both Kane's goals, was injured and didn't play in the third for Chicago while Patrice Bergeron also suffered an injury and left the game early for Boston.

"I think it's exciting to be back in that situation again," Kane said. "This is what you work for all year, all summer, when you're training throughout the year at training camp, whatever it may be. This is what you work for, this opportunity. We've got to seize the moment and take advantage of it."

Kane's first goal was the result of a lucky break and great hands. Johnny Oduya's point shot was partially blocked by Dennis Seidenberg in front, breaking the Boston defenseman's stick. The puck trickled toward the goal where Kane, off to the side, brought it quickly from behind the goal line out front and tucked it in before goalie Tuukka Rask could react.

Kane's second was on a similar play as he found himself in the right place at the right time to the side of the Boston goal. This time Bryan Bickell took a shot that Rask stopped, but Bickell got the rebound, took another whack and the puck landed on Kane's stick.

Patrick Kane tucks the puck in from the side of the net to give Chicago a 1–0 lead late in the first period of Game 5.

Stanley Cup Final – Chicago Blackhawks vs. Boston Bruins

85

Patrick Kane scores his second goal of the game early in the second period to make it 2–0 Blackhawks.

Goalie Corey Crawford makes a save as Boston's Carl Soderberg looks for a rebound.

He calmly backhanded the puck in the short side to make it 2–0.

"Sometimes you catch some breaks," Kane said. "I think I was in the right spot at the right time on both goals. I thought I had some other chances, too, I could have scored."

The Blackhawks came out to start the third as though they had already won the game, and the Bruins sensed an opportunity to make a night of it. Zdeno Chara sent a rocket of a shot over Crawford's glove at 3:40 of the third to make it 2–1, and for much of the rest of the period Chicago tried to sit on the lead, a dangerous strategy at best.

However, in the final minute with Rask on the bench, Dave Bolland found the empty net to finish the scoring and give Chicago a 3–2 series lead. Just five days earlier the Blackhawks had lost home-ice advantage and were reeling. After Game 5, they were confident and in control.

"We've been good at home, and we need to be good at home obviously next game," Boston coach Claude Julien said. "It's as simple as that. Again, there is no panic. You're not going to push us away that easily. We're a committed group, and we plan on bouncing back."

Stanley Cup Final – Chicago Blackhawks vs. Boston Bruins

87

GAME SIX — JUNE 24, 2013
Chicago 3 at Boston 2
Chicago wins Stanley Cup 4–2

The Boston Bruins were determined to force a Game 7 but the Chicago Blackhawks just a bit more determined not to allow that to happen, and thanks to two late goals the visitors managed to turn defeat into Stanley Cup victory. Bryan Bickell tied the game with goalie Corey Crawford on the bench, and 17 seconds later Dave Bolland snapped a rebound into the net with only 58.3 seconds left in regulation time to give Chicago a stunning victory before a silent Boston crowd.

It was a game of big hits and playing through injury, sensational goaltending and incredible emotion, but in the end the Blackhawks' tenacity and determination was just that little bit more than the Bruins.

Boston got the early goal to keep the home crowd energized. Chris Kelly took a pass from Tyler Seguin and scored from in close at 7:19, and the Bruins followed with an intimidating shift immediately after. They had the only two power plays of the opening period, but Crawford was the best player on ice and kept the Blackhawks in the game.

Captain Jonathan Toews, who was injured midway through Game 5 and was uncertain about playing until game time, tied the game on a great play. Playing short-handed, he took the puck down the right wing, and just as the Blackhawks returned to full strength Toews snapped a quick shot between Tuukka Rask's legs to make it 1–1.

The game settled into a war of nerves and tense moments alternating with thrilling flow up and down the ice, and by the third period the game felt like it

Jonathan Toews scores the game-tying goal in the second period, beating Tuukka Rask between the legs.

was in overtime. Milan Lucic scored with fewer than eight minutes to go on a forced giveaway. Duncan Keith passed the puck behind his own goal only to see Boston's David Krejci right there. Krejci put the puck in front and Lucic batted it down and swatted it in.

That goal certainly felt like it would force a Game 7, but the Blackhawks refused to say die. With a minute and a half left, Crawford came to the bench as Patrick Kane rushed the puck over the line. Toews got the puck behind the goal and made a sensational pass in front to Bickell, and his quick shot beat Rask and stunned the crowd.

That was nothing compared to what happened next. Off the next faceoff the Blackhawks brought the puck in again, and a quick shot from the point hit the post and landed on the stick of Bolland behind Rask. Bolland had an easy chip to score the Cup-winning goal.

Bryan Bickell's goal with Corey Crawford on the bench tied the game, 2–2, and set the stage for a miracle ending for the Blackhawks.

Stanley Cup Final – Chicago Blackhawks vs. Boston Bruins

89

The Blackhawks pour off the bench to mob goalie Corey Crawford at the end of the game, celebrating the team's second Cup win in four years.

Left: Conn Smythe Trophy–winner Patrick Kane hoists the Cup for the second time in his young career.

Below: The Blackhawks stunned the Bruins with two goals 17 seconds apart in the final minute-and-a-half to turn a 2–1 deficit into a 3–2 victory.

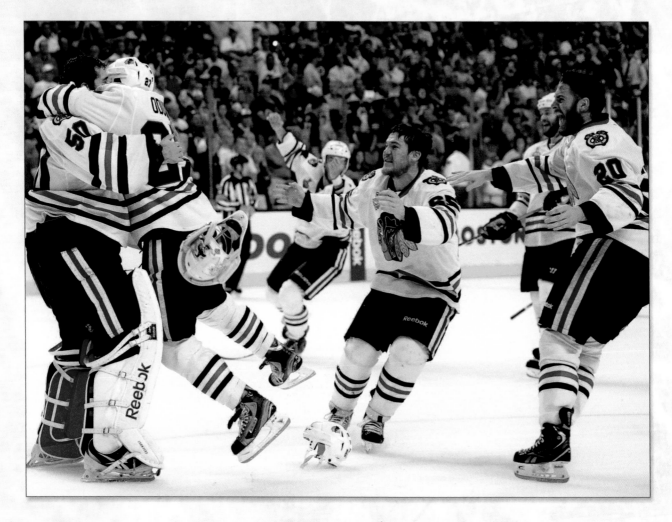

Above: The traditional on-ice portrait for the 2013 Stanley Cup champion Blackhawks.

Left: Patrick Kane (middle) celebrates with Daniel Carcillo (left) and goalie Corey Crawford.

Stanley Cup Final – Chicago Blackhawks vs. Boston Bruins

93

2013 Conn Smythe Trophy: *Patrick Kane*

Patrick Kane is still only 24 years old but his list of accomplishments is growing every year. He scored the Stanley Cup-winning goal for Chicago in 2010, and in 2013 he led the team in scoring with 19 points and was named winner of the Conn Smythe Trophy as playoff MVP.

Kane's performance in 2013 was punctuated by two noteworthy moments. He scored a hat trick in Game 5 against Los Angeles, including the series winner in overtime, to send the Blackhawks to the Cup Final.

Then, in Game 5 of the ultimate series against Boston, he scored two goals in the critical 3–1 win that set up Chicago's Cup victory two nights later.

But perhaps what was most impressive of Kane in 2013 was the maturity of his game, on ice and off. He became a leader on the team, showed discipline when necessary, and produced big goals when the team needed them the most. The Patrick Kane of 2013 developed into a complete player, a playoff performer, and a two-time Stanley Cup champion.

Patrick Kane becomes just the second Blackhawks player to be named MVP of the playoffs after captain Jonathan Toews in 2010.

Team History

Looking back is always easier than considering the present. Take 1944, for instance. The Hawks advanced to the Stanley Cup Final, losing in four straight games to Montreal after finishing third in the regular-season standings. But who could have known then that over the next 14 years, the Hawks would make the playoffs only twice? It wasn't until the latter part of the 1950s that they started to put the pieces together to create another Cup contender.

The Hawks signed three young stars, Bobby Hull, Stan Mikita, and Pierre Pilote, and added veterans Ted Lindsay and Glenn Hall. These players formed the nucleus of a great team, but just as had been the case back in 1944, it was the Canadiens that always stood in the Hawks' way. Montreal won the Cup five years running, 1956 to 1960, and the last two wins in 1959 and 1960 were against Chicago.

The 1960–61 season seemed no different, although the Habs had lost their great leader and scorer, Maurice Richard, to retirement. Nevertheless, the Canadiens finished first overall in the standings, some 17 points ahead of Chicago.

The Hawks were led by Calder Trophy winner Bill Hay, who had 61 points, and Bobby Hull had 31 goals and 56 points. Goalie Hall played all 70 games and 4,200 minutes for Chicago in the regular season as well as all 12 games an 772 minutes in the playoffs.

The Hawks and Habs met in the semi-finals of the 1961 playoffs, and this time the Hawks prevailed in six games. Another fortuitous occurrence happened in the other semi-final when underdog Detroit eliminated favored Toronto, setting up a Detroit–Chicago Cup Final that was most unexpected.

The 1961 final schedule was unique. Every game alternated between cities, so rather than the traditional best-of-seven format of two home games for each side before alternating for the last three games, the teams switched between the Stadium in Chicago (which had home-ice advantage) and the Olympia in Detroit for each game.

As it turned out, the home team won each of the first five games, and then in Game 6, in Detroit, the Hawks won the Cup with a 5–1 road victory. It was their last Cup victory until 2010, the longest drought in NHL history.

Chicago beat Detroit, 5–1, in Game 6 of the 1961 Final to win the Stanley Cup, its last before 2010.

It's much easier to look back than to look ahead, and much more relaxing to know what has happened than to sit on the edge of one's seat and wonder what will happen next. So, although the 2010 play-offs progressed with great equanimity for the Blackhawks, few could know day by day as the "second season" rolled along that they would face so little adversity en route to their first Stanley Cup in nearly half a century.

The Blackhawks faced only four critical moments in the 2010 playoffs. The first came in their opening game, a 4–1 loss to Nashville at the United Center that gave the Predators home-ice advantage. The Blackhawks responded with a win in their next game. Nashville then won Game 3 at home to take a 2–1 lead in the series, still with the advantage, and Chicago responded by winning the next three games and eliminating its adversaries in impressive fashion.

The third test came in the next round when they again lost the opening game of the series on home ice, this time an emphatic 5–1 thumping by Vancouver. The Blackhawks won the next three games and eliminated the Canucks in six.

The last and most critical test came in the Stanley Cup Final against Philadelphia. This time, Chicago won both its games at home, but when the series turned to Philadelphia, the Flyers came to life, winning two games to tie the series. Game 5 was critical for the Blackhawks. A Chicago loss at the Madhouse on Madison would mean the Flyers could go home to clinch the Cup. The Blackhawks responded well again, scoring the only three goals of the opening period, chasing goalie Michael Leighton off the ice, and skating to a huge 7–4 win. They closed out the series three nights later in Pennsylvania to win their first Cup since 1961.

Between exhibition, regular season, and playoff games, Chicago played 110 contests in the 2009–10 season. The Blackhawks' season started with four games in Europe, the first an exhibition against Davos, a Swiss team. That was followed by the Blackhawks' participation in the Victoria Cup against Zurich. Chicago then traveled to Helsinki to open the regular NHL season with two games against Florida (a win and a loss) before returning home to the grind of 80 more games. They finished second overall with 42 wins and 112 points, behind only Washington in both categories (54, 121), but more importantly, they peaked at the right time under head coach Joel Quenneville.

After winning the Stanley Cup, the players all returned to Chicago and then took their own fans on a joyous and wild ride, culminating in a parade unlike anything the city had ever seen. And perhaps most important for the game, the Blackhawks played an exciting style that featured skating and skill, goals and speed, and high-octane offense.

Blackhawks captain Jonathan Toews kisses the Cup after hoisting it in the spring of 2010.

The Blackhawks hosted the second-ever NHL Winter Classic. The game, played at Wrigley Field on January 1, 2009, saw the hosts drop a 6–4 decision to the visiting Detroit Red Wings before a crowd of 40,818.

The Blackhawks were up 3–1 at the end of the first period and adapted to their unfamiliar surroundings better than the Red Wings, but in the second period it was all Detroit. Jiri Hudler scored two of their three goals, and after 40 minutes it was 4–3 for the Red Wings. Detroit went ahead 6–3 before a late goal made the score a little closer.

Further history will be made on March 1, 2014, when the Blackhawks play another outdoor game, this time against the Pittsburgh Penguins as part of the 2014 Coors Light NHL Stadium Series. That game will be played at Soldier Field, home of the NFL's Chicago Bears.

Venerable Wrigley Field was transformed into a shinny rink mid-winter for the 2009 Bridgestone NHL Winter Classic.

Game action at ice level reveals the ballpark and makeshift rink in all its splendor.

Detroit's Pavel Datsyuk and Chicago's Jonathan Toews display their vintage uniforms during the outdoor game won by the Red Wings, 6–4.

Soldier Field, the home of the NFL's Chicago Bears, will be transformed into an ice rink for the 2014 Coors Light NHL Stadium Series.

The Blackhawks took over the Cubs' clubhouse for the 2009 Bridgestone NHL Winter Classic.

The 2009 Bridgestone NHL Winter Classic

Year	GP	W	L	T	GF	GA	Pts
1926–27	44	19	22	3	115	116	41
1927–28	44	7	34	3	68	134	17
1928–29	44	7	29	8	33	85	22
1929–30	44	21	18	5	117	111	47
1930–31	44	24	17	3	108	78	51
1931–32	48	18	19	11	86	101	47
1932–33	48	16	20	12	88	101	44
1933–34	48	20	17	11	88	53	51
1934–35	48	26	17	5	118	88	57
1935–36	48	21	19	8	93	92	50
1936–37	48	14	27	7	99	131	35
1937–38	48	14	25	9	97	139	37
1938–39	48	12	28	8	91	132	32
1939–40	48	23	19	6	112	120	52
1940–41	48	16	25	7	112	139	39
1941–42	48	22	23	3	145	155	47
1942–43	50	17	18	15	179	180	49
1943–44	50	22	23	5	178	187	49
1944–45	50	13	30	7	141	194	33
1945–46	50	23	20	7	200	178	53
1946–47	60	19	37	4	193	274	42
1947–48	60	20	34	6	195	225	46
1948–49	60	21	31	8	173	211	50
1949–50	70	22	38	10	203	244	54
1950–51	70	13	47	10	171	280	36
1951–52	70	17	44	9	158	241	43
1952–53	70	27	28	15	169	175	69
1953–54	70	12	51	7	133	242	31
1954–55	70	13	40	17	161	235	43
1955–56	70	19	39	12	155	216	50
1956–57	70	16	39	15	169	225	47
1957–58	70	24	39	7	163	202	55
1958–59	70	28	29	13	197	208	69
1959–60	70	28	29	13	191	180	69
1960–61	70	29	24	17	198	180	75
1961–62	70	31	26	13	217	186	75
1962–63	70	32	21	17	194	178	81
1963–64	70	36	22	12	218	169	84

Year	GP	W	L	T	GF	GA	Pts
1964–65	70	34	28	8	224	176	76
1965–66	70	37	25	8	240	187	82
1966–67	70	41	17	12	262	170	94
1967–68	74	32	26	16	212	222	80
1968–69	76	34	33	9	280	246	77
1969–70	76	45	22	9	250	170	99
1970–71	78	49	20	9	277	184	107
1971–72	78	46	17	15	256	166	107
1972–73	78	42	27	9	284	225	93
1973–74	78	41	14	23	272	164	105
1974–75	80	37	35	8	268	241	82
1975–76	80	32	30	18	254	261	82
1976–77	80	26	43	11	240	298	63
1977–78	80	32	29	19	230	220	83
1978–79	80	29	36	15	244	277	73
1979–80	80	34	27	19	241	250	87
1980–81	80	31	33	16	304	315	78
1981–82	80	30	38	12	332	363	72
1982–83	80	47	23	10	338	268	104
1983–84	80	30	42	8	277	311	68
1984–85	80	38	35	7	309	299	83
1985–86	80	39	33	8	351	349	86
1986–87	80	29	37	14	290	310	72
1987–88	80	30	41	9	284	328	69
1988–89	80	27	41	12	297	335	66
1989–90	80	41	33	6	316	294	88
1990–91	80	49	23	8	284	211	106
1991–92	80	36	29	15	257	236	87
1992–93	84	47	25	12	279	230	106
1993–94	84	39	36	9	254	240	87
1994–95	48	24	19	5	156	115	53
1995–96	82	40	28	14	273	220	94
1996–97	82	34	35	13	223	210	81
1997–98	82	30	39	13	192	199	73
1998–99	82	29	41	12	202	248	70
1999–2000	82	33	37	10	242	245	78
2000–01	82	29	40	8	190	233	71
2001–02	82	41	27	13	216	207	96

Year	GP	W	L	T	GF	GA	Pts
2002–03	82	30	33	13	207	226	79
2003–04	82	20	43	11	188	259	59
2004–05			No Season				
2005–06	82	26	43	13	211	285	65
2006–07	82	31	42	9	201	258	71
2007–08	82	40	34	8	239	235	88
2008–09	82	46	24	12	264	216	104
2009–10	82	52	22	8	271	209	112
2010–11	82	44	29	9	258	225	97
2011–12	82	45	26	11	248	238	101
2012–13	48	36	7	5	155	102	77

The Blackhawks finished first overall in 2012–13 with 36 wins and 77 points in 48 games.

1927

QUARTERFINALS
March 29   Boston 6 at Chicago 1
March 31   Chicago 4 at Boston 4
Boston won total-goals series 10–5

1930

QUARTERFINALS
March 23   Montreal 1 at Chicago 0
March 26   Chicago 2 at Montreal 2 (OT)
Montreal won total-goals series 3–2

1931

QUARTERFINALS
March 24   Chicago 2 at Toronto 2
March 26   Toronto 1 at Chicago 2 (OT)
Chicago won total-goals series 4–3

SEMIFINALS
March 29   NY Rangers 0 at Chicago 2
March 31   Chicago 1 at NY Rangers 0
Chicago won total-goals series 3–0

STANLEY CUP FINAL
April 3   Montreal 2 at Chicago 1
April 5   Montreal 1 at Chicago 2 (OT)
April 9   Chicago 3 at Montreal 2 (OT)
April 11   Chicago 2 at Montreal 4
April 14   Chicago 0 at Montreal 2
Montreal won best-of-five 3–2

1932

QUARTERFINALS
March 27   Toronto 0 at Chicago 1
March 29   Chicago 1 at Toronto 6
Toronto won total-goals series 6–2

1934

QUARTERFINALS
March 22   Chicago 3 at Montreal 2
March 25   Montreal 1 at Chicago 1 (OT)
Chicago won total-goals series 4–3

SEMIFINALS
March 28   Chicago 3 at Maroons 0
April 1   Maroons 2 at Chicago 3
Chicago won total-goals series 6–2

STANLEY CUP FINAL
April 3   Chicago 2 at Detroit 1 (OT)
April 5   Chicago 4 at Detroit 1
April 8   Detroit 5 at Chicago 2
April 10   Detroit 0 at Chicago 1 (OT)
Chicago won Stanley Cup final 3–1

1935

QUARTERFINALS
March 23   Chicago 0 at Montreal Maroons 0
March 26   Montreal Maroons 1 at Chicago 0
Montreal Maroons won total-goals series 1–0

1936

QUARTERFINALS
March 24   Chicago 0 at NY Americans 3
March 26   NY Americans 4 at Chicago 5
Americans won total-goals series 7–5

1938

QUARTERFINALS
March 22   Chicago 4 at Montreal 6
March 24   Montreal 0 at Chicago 4
March 26   Chicago 3 at Montreal 2 (OT)
Chicago won best-of-three 2–1

SEMIFINALS
March 29   Chicago 1 at NY Americans 3
March 31   NY Americans 0 at Chicago 1 (OT)
April 3   Chicago 3 at NY Americans 2
Chicago won best-of-three 2–1

STANLEY CUP FINAL
April 5   Chicago 3 at Toronto 1
April 7   Chicago 1 at Toronto 5
April 10   Toronto 1 at Chicago 2
April 12   Toronto 1 at Chicago 4
Chicago won Stanley Cup final 3–1

1940

QUARTERFINALS
March 19   Chicago 2 at Toronto 3 (OT)
March 21   Toronto 2 at Chicago 1
Toronto won best-of-three 2–0

1941

QUARTERFINALS
March 20   Montreal 1 at Chicago 2
March 22   Chicago 3 at Montreal 4 (OT)
March 25   Montreal 2 at Chicago 3
Chicago won best-of-three 2–1

SEMIFINALS
March 27   Chicago 1 at Detroit 3
March 30   Detroit 2 at Chicago 1 (OT)
Detroit won best-of-three 2–0

1942

QUARTERFINALS
March 22   Boston 2 at Chicago 1 (OT)
March 24   Chicago 4 at Boston 0
March 26   Chicago 2 at Boston 3
Boston won best-of-three 2–1

1944

SEMIFINALS
March 21   Chicago 2 at Detroit 1
March 23   Chicago 1 at Detroit 4
March 26   Detroit 0 at Chicago 2
March 28   Detroit 1 at Chicago 7
March 30   Chicago 5 at Detroit 2
Chicago won best-of-seven 4–1

STANLEY CUP FINAL
April 4   Chicago 1 at Montreal 5
April 7   Montreal 3 at Chicago 1
April 9   Montreal 3 at Chicago 2
April 13   Chicago 4 at Montreal 5 (OT)
Montreal won best-of-seven 4–0

1946

SEMIFINALS
March 19   Chicago 2 at Montreal 6
March 21   Chicago 1 at Montreal 5
March 24   Montreal 8 at Chicago 2
March 26   Montreal 7 at Chicago 2
Montreal won best-of-seven 4–0

1953

SEMIFINALS
March 24   Chicago 1 at Montreal 3
March 26   Chicago 3 at Montreal 4
March 29   Montreal 1 at Chicago 2 (OT)
March 31   Montreal 1 at Chicago 3
April 2   Chicago 4 at Montreal 2
April 4   Montreal 3 at Chicago 0
April 7   Chicago 1 at Montreal 4
Montreal won best-of-seven 4–3

1959

SEMIFINALS
March 24   Chicago 2 at Montreal 4
March 26   Chicago 1 at Montreal 5
March 28   Montreal 2 at Chicago 4
March 31   Montreal 1 at Chicago 3
April 2   Chicago 2 at Montreal 4
April 4   Montreal 5 at Chicago 4
Montreal won best-of-seven 4–2

1960

SEMIFINALS
March 24   Chicago 3 at Montreal 4
March 26   Chicago 3 at Montreal 4 (OT)
March 29   Montreal 4 at Chicago 0
March 31   Montreal 2 at Chicago 0
Montreal won best-of-seven 4–0

1961

SEMIFINALS
March 21   Chicago 2 at Montreal 6
March 23   Chicago 4 at Montreal 3
March 26   Montreal 1 at Chicago 2 (OT)
March 28   Montreal 5 at Chicago 2
April 1   Chicago 3 at Montreal 0
April 4   Montreal 0 at Chicago 3
Chicago won best-of-seven 4–2

STANLEY CUP FINAL
April 6   Detroit 2 at Chicago 3
April 8   Chicago 1 at Detroit 3
April 10   Detroit 1 at Chicago 3
April 12   Chicago 1 at Detroit 2
April 14   Detroit 3 at Chicago 6
April 16   Chicago 5 at Detroit 1
Chicago won Stanley Cup final 4–2

1962

SEMIFINALS
March 27   Chicago 1 at Montreal 2
March 29   Chicago 3 at Montreal 4
April 1   Montreal 1 at Chicago 4
April 3   Montreal 3 at Chicago 5
April 5   Chicago 4 at Montreal 3
April 8   Montreal 0 at Chicago 2
Chicago won best-of-seven 4–2

STANLEY CUP FINAL
April 10   Chicago 1 at Toronto 4
April 12   Chicago 2 at Toronto 3
April 15   Toronto 0 at Chicago 3
April 17   Toronto 1 at Chicago 4
April 19   Chicago 4 at Toronto 8
April 22   Toronto 2 at Chicago 1
Toronto won Stanley Cup final 4–2

1963

SEMIFINALS
March 26	Detroit 4 at Chicago 5
March 28	Detroit 2 at Chicago 5
March 31	Chicago 2 at Detroit 4
April 2	Chicago 1 at Detroit 4
April 4	Detroit 4 at Chicago 2
April 7	Chicago 4 at Detroit 7

Detroit won best-of-seven 4–2

1964

SEMIFINALS
March 26	Detroit 1 at Chicago 4
March 29	Detroit 5 at Chicago 4
March 31	Chicago 0 at Detroit 3
April 2	Chicago 3 at Detroit 2 (OT)
April 5	Detroit 2 at Chicago 3
April 7	Chicago 2 at Detroit 7
April 9	Detroit 4 at Chicago 2

Detroit won best-of-seven 4–3

1965

SEMIFINALS
April 1	Chicago 3 at Detroit 4
April 4	Chicago 3 at Detroit 6
April 6	Detroit 2 at Chicago 5
April 8	Detroit 1 at Chicago 2
April 11	Chicago 2 at Detroit 4
April 13	Detroit 0 at Chicago 4
April 15	Chicago 4 at Detroit 2

Chicago won best-of-seven 4–3

STANLEY CUP FINAL
April 17	Chicago 2 at Montreal 3
April 20	Chicago 0 at Montreal 2
April 22	Montreal 1 at Chicago 3
April 25	Montreal 1 at Chicago 5
April 27	Chicago 0 at Montreal 6
April 29	Montreal 1 at Chicago 2
May 1	Chicago 0 at Montreal 4

Montreal won best-of-seven 4–3

1966

SEMIFINALS
April 7	Detroit 1 at Chicago 2
April 10	Detroit 7 at Chicago 0
April 12	Chicago 2 at Detroit 1
April 14	Chicago 1 at Detroit 5
April 17	Detroit 5 at Chicago 3
April 19	Chicago 2 at Detroit 3

Detroit won best-of-seven 4–2

1967

SEMIFINALS
April 6	Toronto 2 at Chicago 5
April 9	Toronto 3 at Chicago 1
April 11	Chicago 1 at Toronto 3
April 13	Chicago 4 at Toronto 3
April 15	Toronto 4 at Chicago 2
April 18	Chicago 1 at Toronto 3

Toronto won best-of-seven 4–2

1968

QUARTERFINALS
April 4	Chicago 1 at Rangers 3
April 9	Chicago 1 at Rangers 2
April 11	Rangers 4 at Chicago 7
April 13	Rangers 1 at Chicago 3
April 14	Chicago 2 at Rangers 1
April 16	Rangers 1 at Chicago 4

Chicago won best-of-seven 4–2

SEMIFINALS
April 18	Chicago 2 at Montreal 9
April 20	Chicago 1 at Montreal 4
April 23	Montreal 4 at Chicago 2
April 25	Montreal 1 at Chicago 2
April 28	Chicago 3 at Montreal 4 (OT)

Montreal won best-of-seven 4–1

1970

QUARTERFINALS
April 8	Detroit 2 at Chicago 4
April 9	Detroit 2 at Chicago 4
April 11	Chicago 4 at Detroit 2
April 12	Chicago 4 at Detroit 2

Chicago won best-of-seven 4–0

SEMIFINALS
April 19	Boston 6 at Chicago 3
April 21	Boston 4 at Chicago 1
April 23	Chicago 2 at Boston 5
April 26	Chicago 4 at Boston 5

Boston won best-of-seven 4–0

1971

QUARTERFINALS
April 7	Philadelphia 2 at Chicago 5
April 8	Philadelphia 2 at Chicago 6
April 10	Chicago 3 at Philadelphia 2
April 11	Chicago 6 at Philadelphia 2

Chicago won best-of-seven 4–0

SEMIFINALS
April 18	Rangers 2 at Chicago 1 (OT)
April 20	Rangers 0 at Chicago 3
April 22	Chicago 1 at Rangers 4
April 25	Chicago 7 at Rangers 1
April 27	Rangers 2 at Chicago 3 (OT)
April 29	Chicago 2 at Rangers 3 (OT)
May 2	Rangers 2 at Chicago 4

Chicago won best-of-seven 4–3

STANLEY CUP FINAL
May 4	Montreal 1 at Chicago 2 (OT)
May 6	Montreal 3 at Chicago 5
May 9	Chicago 2 at Montreal 4
May 11	Chicago 2 at Montreal 5
May 13	Montreal 0 at Chicago 2
May 16	Chicago 3 at Montreal 4
May 18	Montreal 3 at Chicago 2

Montreal won best-of-seven 4–3

1972

QUARTERFINALS
April 5	Pittsburgh 1 at Chicago 3
April 6	Pittsburgh 2 at Chicago 3
April 8	Chicago 2 at Pittsburgh 0
April 9	Chicago 6 at Pittsburgh 5 (OT)

Chicago won best-of-seven 4–0

SEMIFINALS
April 16	NY Rangers 3 at Chicago 2
April 18	NY Rangers 5 at Chicago 3
April 20	Chicago 2 at NY Rangers 3
April 23	Chicago 2 at NY Rangers 6

NY Rangers won best-of-seven 4–0

1973

QUARTERFINALS
April 4	St. Louis 1 at Chicago 7
April 5	St. Louis 0 at Chicago 1
April 7	Chicago 5 at St. Louis 2
April 8	Chicago 3 at St. Louis 5
April 10	St. Louis 1 at Chicago 6

Chicago won best-of-seven 4–1

SEMIFINALS
April 12	NY Rangers 4 at Chicago 1
April 15	NY Rangers 4 at Chicago 5
April 17	Chicago 2 at NY Rangers 1
April 19	Chicago 3 at NY Rangers 1
April 24	NY Rangers 1 at Chicago 4

Chicago won best-of-seven 4–1

STANLEY CUP FINAL
April 29	Chicago 3 at Montreal 8
May 1	Chicago 1 at Montreal 4
May 3	Montreal 4 at Chicago 7
May 6	Montreal 4 at Chicago 0
May 8	Chicago 8 at Montreal 7
May 10	Montreal 6 at Chicago 4

Montreal won best-of-seven 4–2

1974

QUARTERFINALS
April 10	Los Angeles 1 at Chicago 3
April 11	Los Angeles 1 at Chicago 4
April 13	Chicago 1 at Los Angeles 0
April 14	Chicago 1 at Los Angeles 5
April 16	Los Angeles 0 at Chicago 1

Chicago won best-of-seven 4–1

SEMIFINALS
April 18	Chicago 4 at Boston 2
April 21	Chicago 6 at Boston 8
April 23	Boston 3 at Chicago 4 (OT)
April 25	Boston 5 at Chicago 2
April 28	Chicago 2 at Boston 6
April 30	Boston 4 at Chicago 2

Boston won best-of-seven 4–2

1975

PRELIMINARY ROUND
April 8	Chicago 2 at Boston 8
April 10	Boston 3 at Chicago 4 (OT)
April 11	Chicago 6 at Boston 4

Chicago won best-of-three 2–1

QUARTERFINALS
April 13	Chicago 1 at Buffalo 4
April 15	Chicago 1 at Buffalo 3
April 17	Buffalo 4 at Chicago 5 (OT)
April 20	Buffalo 6 at Chicago 2
April 22	Chicago 1 at Buffalo 3

Buffalo won best-of-seven 4–1

1976

QUARTERFINALS

April 11	Chicago 0 at Montreal 4
April 13	Chicago 1 at Montreal 3
April 15	Montreal 2 at Chicago 1
April 18	Montreal 4 at Chicago 1

Montreal won best-of-seven 4–0

1977

PRELIMINARY ROUND

April 10	Chicago 2 at NY Islanders 5
April 11	NY Islanders 2 at Chicago 1

NY Islanders won best-of-three 2–0

1978

QUARTERFINALS

April 17	Chicago 1 at Boston 6
April 19	Chicago 3 at Boston 4 (OT)
April 21	Boston 4 at Chicago 3 (OT)
April 23	Boston 5 at Chicago 2

Boston won best-of-seven 4–0

1979

QUARTERFINALS

April 16	Chicago 2 at NY Islanders 6
April 18	Chicago 0 at NY Islanders 1 (OT)
April 20	NY Islanders 4 at Chicago 0
April 22	NY Islanders 3 at Chicago 1

NY Islanders won best-of-seven 4–0

1980

PRELIMINARY ROUND

April 10	St. Louis 2 at Chicago 3 (OT)
April 11	St. Louis 1 at Chicago 5
April 13	Chicago 4 at St. Louis 1

Chicago won best-of-five 3–0

QUARTERFINALS

April 16	Chicago 0 at Buffalo 5
April 17	Chicago 4 at Buffalo 6
April 19	Buffalo 2 at Chicago 1
April 20	Buffalo 3 at Chicago 2

Buffalo won best-of-seven 4–0

1981

PRELIMINARY ROUND

April 8	Chicago 3 at Calgary 4
April 9	Chicago 2 at Calgary 6
April 11	Calgary 5 at Chicago 4 (OT)

Calgary won best-of-five 3–0

1982

DIVISION SEMIFINALS

April 7	Chicago 3 at Minnesota 2 (OT)
April 8	Chicago 5 at Minnesota 3
April 10	Minnesota 7 at Chicago 1
April 11	Minnesota 2 at Chicago 5

Chicago won best-of-five 3–1

DIVISION FINALS

April 15	Chicago 5 at St. Louis 4
April 16	Chicago 1 at St. Louis 3
April 18	St. Louis 5 at Chicago 6
April 19	St. Louis 4 at Chicago 7
April 21	Chicago 2 at St. Louis 3 (OT)
April 23	St. Louis 0 at Chicago 2

Chicago won best-of-seven 4–2

CONFERENCE FINALS

April 27	Vancouver 2 at Chicago 1 (OT)
April 29	Vancouver 1 at Chicago 4
May 1	Chicago 3 at Vancouver 4
May 4	Chicago 3 at Vancouver 5
May 6	Vancouver 6 at Chicago 2

Vancouver won best-of-seven 4–1

1983

DIVISION SEMIFINALS

April 6	St. Louis 4 at Chicago 2
April 7	St. Louis 2 at Chicago 7
April 9	Chicago 2 at St. Louis 1
April 10	Chicago 5 at St. Louis 3

Chicago won best-of-five 3–1

DIVISION FINALS

April 14	Minnesota 2 at Chicago 5
April 15	Minnesota 4 at Chicago 7
April 17	Chicago 1 at Minnesota 5
April 18	Chicago 4 at Minnesota 3 (OT)
April 20	Minnesota 2 at Chicago 5

Chicago won best-of-seven 4–1

CONFERENCE FINALS

April 10	Chicago 4 at Edmonton 8
April 11	Chicago 2 at Edmonton 8
April 13	Edmonton 3 at Chicago 2
April 14	Edmonton 6 at Chicago 3

Edmonton won best-of-seven 4–0

1984

DIVISION SEMIFINALS

April 4	Chicago 3 at Minnesota 1
April 5	Chicago 5 at Minnesota 6
April 7	Minnesota 4 at Chicago 1
April 8	Minnesota 3 at Chicago 4
April 10	Chicago 1 at Minnesota 4

Minnesota won best-of-five 3–2

1985

DIVISION SEMIFINALS

April 10	Detroit 5 at Chicago 9
April 11	Detroit 1 at Chicago 6
April 13	Chicago 8 at Detroit 2

Chicago won best-of-five 3–0

DIVISION FINALS

April 18	Minnesota 8 at Chicago 5
April 21	Minnesota 2 at Chicago 6
April 23	Chicago 5 at Minnesota 3
April 25	Chicago 7 at Minnesota 6 (OT)
April 28	Minnesota 5 at Chicago 4 (OT)
April 30	Chicago 6 at Minnesota 5 (OT)

Chicago won best-of-seven 4–2

CONFERENCE FINALS

May 4	Chicago 2 at Edmonton 11
May 7	Chicago 3 at Edmonton 7
May 9	Edmonton 2 at Chicago 5
May 12	Edmonton 6 at Chicago 8
May 14	Chicago 5 at Edmonton 10
May 16	Edmonton 8 at Chicago 2

Edmonton won best-of-seven 4–2

1986

DIVISION SEMIFINALS

April 9	Toronto 5 at Chicago 3
April 10	Toronto 6 at Chicago 4
April 12	Chicago 2 at Toronto 7

Toronto won best-of-five 3–0

1987

DIVISION SEMIFINALS

April 8	Chicago 1 at Detroit 3
April 9	Chicago 1 at Detroit 5
April 11	Detroit 4 at Chicago 3 (OT)
April 12	Detroit 3 at Chicago 1

Detroit won best-of-seven 4–0

1988

DIVISION SEMIFINALS

April 6	Chicago 1 at St. Louis 4
April 7	Chicago 2 at St. Louis 3
April 9	St. Louis 3 at Chicago 6
April 10	St. Louis 6 at Chicago 5
April 12	Chicago 3 at St. Louis 5

St. Louis won best-of-seven 4–1

1989

DIVISION SEMIFINALS

April 5	Chicago 2 at Detroit 3
April 6	Chicago 5 at Detroit 4 (OT)
April 8	Detroit 2 at Chicago 4
April 9	Detroit 2 at Chicago 3
April 11	Chicago 4 at Detroit 6
April 13	Detroit 1 at Chicago 7

Chicago won best-of-seven 4–2

DIVISION FINALS

April 18	Chicago 3 at St. Louis 1
April 20	Chicago 4 at St. Louis 5 (OT)
April 22	St. Louis 2 at Chicago 5
April 24	St. Louis 2 at Chicago 3
April 26	Chicago 4 at St. Louis 2

Chicago won best-of-seven 4–1

CONFERENCE FINALS

May 2	Chicago 0 at Calgary 3
May 4	Chicago 4 at Calgary 2
May 6	Calgary 5 at Chicago 2
May 8	Calgary 2 at Chicago 1 (OT)
May 10	Chicago 1 at Calgary 3

Calgary won best-of-seven 4–1

1990

DIVISION SEMIFINALS

April 4	Minnesota 2 at Chicago 1
April 6	Minnesota 3 at Chicago 5
April 8	Chicago 2 at Minnesota 1
April 10	Chicago 0 at Minnesota 4
April 12	Minnesota 1 at Chicago 5
April 14	Chicago 3 at Minnesota 5
April 16	Minnesota 2 at Chicago 5

Chicago won best-of-seven 4–3

DIVISION FINALS
April 10   St. Louis 4 at Chicago 3
April 11   St. Louis 3 at Chicago 5
April 13   Chicago 4 at St. Louis 5
April 14   Chicago 3 at St. Louis 2
April 16   St. Louis 2 at Chicago 3
April 30   Chicago 2 at St. Louis 4
April 30   St. Louis 2 at Chicago 8
Chicago won best-of-seven 4–3

CONFERENCE FINALS
May 2   Chicago 2 at Edmonton 5
May 4   Chicago 4 at Edmonton 3
May 6   Edmonton 1 at Chicago 5
May 8   Edmonton 4 at Chicago 2
May 10   Chicago 3 at Edmonton 4
May 12   Edmonton 8 at Chicago 4
Edmonton won best-of-seven 4–2

1991
DIVISION SEMIFINALS
April 4   Minnesota 4 at Chicago 3 (OT)
April 6   Minnesota 2 at Chicago 5
April 8   Chicago 6 at Minnesota 5
April 10   Chicago 1 at Minnesota 3
April 12   Minnesota 6 at Chicago 0
April 14   Chicago 1 at Minnesota 3
Minnesota won best-of-seven 4–2

1992
DIVISION SEMIFINALS
April 18   St. Louis 1 at Chicago 3
April 20   St. Louis 5 at Chicago 3
April 22   Chicago 4 at St. Louis 5 (OT)
April 24   Chicago 5 at St. Louis 3
April 26   St. Louis 6 at Chicago 4
April 28   Chicago 2 at St. Louis 1
Chicago won best-of-seven 4–2

DIVISION FINALS
May 2   Chicago 2 at Detroit 1
May 4   Chicago 3 at Detroit 1
May 6   Detroit 4 at Chicago 5
May 8   Detroit 0 at Chicago 1
Chicago won best-of-seven 4–0

CONFERENCE FINALS
May 16   Edmonton 2 at Chicago 8
May 18   Edmonton 2 at Chicago 4
May 20   Chicago 4 at Edmonton 3 (OT)
May 22   Chicago 5 at Edmonton 1
Chicago won best-of-seven 4–0

STANLEY CUP FINAL
May 26   Chicago 4 at Pittsburgh 5
May 28   Chicago 1 at Pittsburgh 3
May 30   Pittsburgh 1 at Chicago 0
June 1   Pittsburgh 6 at Chicago 5
Pittsburgh won best-of-seven 4–0

1993
DIVISION SEMIFINALS
April 18   St. Louis 4 at Chicago 3
April 21   St. Louis 2 at Chicago 0
April 23   Chicago 0 at St. Louis 3
April 25   Chicago 3 at St. Louis 4 (OT)
St. Louis won best-of-seven 4–0

1994
CONFERENCE QUARTERFINALS
April 18   Chicago 1 at Toronto 5
April 20   Chicago 0 at Toronto 1 (OT)
April 23   Toronto 4 at Chicago 5
April 24   Toronto 3 at Chicago 4 (OT)
April 26   Chicago 0 at Toronto 1
April 28   Toronto 1 at Chicago 0
Toronto won best-of-seven 4–2

1995
CONFERENCE QUARTERFINALS
May 7   Toronto 5 at Chicago 3
May 9   Toronto 3 at Chicago 0
May 11   Chicago 3 at Toronto 2
May 13   Chicago 3 at Toronto 1
May 15   Toronto 2 at Chicago 4
May 17   Chicago 4 at Toronto 5 (OT)
May 19   Toronto 2 at Chicago 5
Chicago won best-of-seven 4–3

CONFERENCE SEMIFINALS
May 21   Vancouver 1 at Chicago 2 (OT)
May 23   Vancouver 0 at Chicago 2
May 25   Chicago 3 at Vancouver 2 (OT)
May 27   Chicago 4 at Vancouver 3 (OT)
Chicago won best-of-seven 4–0

CONFERENCE FINALS
June 1   Chicago 1 at Detroit 2 (OT)
June 4   Chicago 2 at Detroit 3
June 6   Detroit 4 at Chicago 3 (OT)
June 8   Detroit 2 at Chicago 5
June 11   Chicago 1 at Detroit 2 (OT)
Detroit won best-of-seven 4–1

1996
CONFERENCE QUARTERFINALS
April 17   Calgary 1 at Chicago 4
April 19   Calgary 0 at Chicago 3
April 21   Chicago 7 at Calgary 5
April 23   Chicago 2 at Calgary 1 (OT)
Chicago won best-of-seven 4–0

CONFERENCE SEMIFINALS
May 2   Chicago 3 at Colorado 2 (OT)
May 4   Chicago 1 at Colorado 5
May 6   Colorado 3 at Chicago 4 (OT)
May 8   Colorado 3 at Chicago 2 (OT)
May 11   Chicago 1 at Colorado 4
May 13   Colorado 4 at Chicago 3 (OT)
Colorado won best-of-seven 4–2

1997
CONFERENCE QUARTERFINALS
April 16   Chicago 0 at Colorado 6
April 18   Chicago 1 at Colorado 3
April 20   Colorado 3 at Chicago 4 (OT)
April 22   Colorado 3 at Chicago 6
April 24   Chicago 0 at Colorado 7
April 26   Colorado 6 at Chicago 3
Colorado won best-of-seven 4–2

2002
CONFERENCE QUARTERFINAL
April 18   Chicago 2 at St. Louis 1
April 20   Chicago 0 at St. Louis 2
April 21   St. Louis 4 at Chicago 0
April 23   St. Louis 1 at Chicago 0
April 25   Chicago 3 at St. Louis 5
St. Louis won best-of-seven 4–1

2010
CONFERENCE QUARTERFINALS
April 16   Nashville 4 at Chicago 1
April 18   Nashville 0 at Chicago 2 [Niemi]
April 20   Chicago 1 at Nashville 4
April 22   Chicago 3 at Nashville 0 [Niemi]
April 24   Nashville 4 at Chicago 5 (Hossa 4:07 OT)
April 26   Chicago 5 at Nashville 3
Chicago won best-of-seven 4–2

CONFERENCE SEMIFINALS
May 1   Vancouver 5 at Chicago 1
May 3   Vancouver 2 at Chicago 4
May 5   Chicago 5 at Vancouver 2
May 7   Chicago 7 at Vancouver 4
May 9   Vancouver 3 at Chicago 1
May 11   Chicago 5 at Vancouver 1
Chicago won best-of-seven 4–2

CONFERENCE FINALS
May 16   Chicago 2 at San Jose 1
May 18   Chicago 4 at San Jose 2
May 21   San Jose 2 at Chicago 3 (Byfuglien 12:24 OT)
May 23   San Jose 2 at Chicago 4
Chicago won best-of-seven 4–0

STANLEY CUP FINAL
May 29   Philadelphia 5 at Chicago 6
May 31   Philadelphia 1 at Chicago 2
June 2   Chicago 3 at Philadelphia 4
June 4   Chicago 3 at Philadelphia 5
June 6   Philadelphia 4 at Chicago 7
June 9   Chicago 4 at Philadelphia 3 (Kane 4:06 OT)
Chicago won Stanley Cup 4–2

2011
CONFERENCE QUARTERFINALS
April 13   Chicago 0 at Vancouver 2
April 15   Chicago 3 at Vancouver 4
April 17   Vancouver 3 at Chicago 2
April 19   Vancouver 2 at Chicago 7
April 21   Chicago 5 at Vancouver 0
April 24   Vancouver 3 at Chicago 4 (OT)
April 26   Chicago 1 at Vancouver 2 (OT)
Vancouver won best-of-seven 4–3

2012
CONFERENCE QUARTERFINALS
April 12   Chicago 2 at Phoenix 3 (OT)
April 14   Chicago 4 at Phoenix 3 (OT)
April 17   Phoenix 3 at Chicago 2 (OT)
April 19   Phoenix 3 at Chicago 2 (OT)
April 21   Chicago 2 at Phoenix 1 (OT)
April 23   Phoenix 4 at Chicago 0
Phoenix won best-of-seven 4–2

Year	Player	Team	Position
1930–31	Charlie Gardiner	First	Goalie
1931–32	Charlie Gardiner	First	Goalie
1932–33	Charlie Gardiner	Second	Goalie
1933–34	Lionel Conacher	First	Defense
	Charlie Gardiner	First	Goalie
1934–35	Lorne Chabot	First	Goalie
	Art Coulter	Second	Defense
1935–36	Earl Seibert	Second	Defense
	Paul Thompson	Second	Left Wing
1936–37	Earl Seibert	Second	Defense
1937–38	Earl Seibert	Second	Defense
1937–38	Paul Thompson	First	Left Wing
1938–39	Johnny Gottselig	Second	Left Wing
	Earl Seibert	Second	Defense
1939–40	Paul Thompson	First	Coach
	Earl Seibert	Second	Defense
1940–41	Earl Seibert	Second	Defense
1941–42	Earl Seibert	First	Defense
	Paul Thompson	Second	Coach
1942–43	Doug Bentley	First	Left Wing
	Earl Seibert	First	Defense
1943–44	Doug Bentley	First	Left Wing
	Earl Seibert	First	Defense
1944–45	Mike Karakas	Second	Goalie
	Bill Mosienko	Second	Right Wing
1945–46	Max Bentley	First	Center
	Johnny Gottselig	Second	Coach
	Bill Mosienko	Second	Right Wing
1946–47	Doug Bentley	First	Left Wing
	Max Bentley	Second	Center
1947–48	Bud Poile	Second	Right Wing
	Gaye Stewart	Second	Left Wing
1948–49	Roy Conacher	First	Left Wing
	Doug Bentley	Second	Center
1952–53	Bill Gadsby	Second	Defense
1953–54	Bill Gadsby	Second	Defense
1956–57	Ed Litzenberger	Second	Center
1957–58	Glenn Hall	First	Goalie
1959–60	Glenn Hall	First	Goalie
	Bobby Hull	First	Left Wing
	Pierre Pilote	Second	Defense
1960–61	Glenn Hall	Second	Goalie
	Pierre Pilote	Second	Defense
1961–62	Bobby Hull	First	Left Wing
	Stan Mikita	First	Center
	Glenn Hall	Second	Goalie
	Pierre Pilote	Second	Defense
1962–63	Glenn Hall	First	Goalie
	Stan Mikita	First	Center
	Pierre Pilote	First	Defense
	Bobby Hull	Second	Left Wing
	Moose Vasko	Second	Defense
1963–64	Glenn Hall	First	Goalie
	Bobby Hull	First	Left Wing
	Stan Mikita	First	Center
	Kenny Wharram	First	Right Wing
	Pierre Pilote	Second	Defense
	Moose Vasko	Second	Defense

Year	Player	Team	Position
1964–65	Bobby Hull	First	Left Wing
	Pierre Pilote	First	Defense
	Stan Mikita	Second	Center
1965–66	Glenn Hall	First	Goalie
	Bobby Hull	First	Left Wing
	Stan Mikita	First	Center
	Pat Stapleton	Second	Defense
1966–67	Bobby Hull	First	Left Wing
	Stan Mikita	First	Center
	Pierre Pilote	First	Defense
	Kenny Wharram	First	Right Wing
	Glenn Hall	Second	Goalie
1967–68	Bobby Hull	First	Left Wing
	Stan Mikita	First	Center
1968–69	Bobby Hull	First	Left Wing
1969–70	Tony Esposito	First	Goalie
	Bobby Hull	First	Left Wing
	Stan Mikita	Second	Center
1970–71	Bobby Hull	Second	Left Wing
	Pat Stapleton	Second	Defense
1971–72	Tony Esposito	First	Goalie
	Bobby Hull	First	Left Wing
	Pat Stapleton	Second	Defense
	Bill White	Second	Defense
1972–73	Tony Esposito	Second	Goalie
	Dennis Hull	Second	Left Wing
	Bill White	Second	Defense
1973–74	Tony Esposito	Second	Goalie
1979–80	Tony Esposito	First	Goalie
1981–82	Doug Wilson	First	Defense
1982–83	Denis Savard	Second	Center
1984–85	Doug Wilson	Second	Defense
1989–90	Doug Wilson	Second	Defense
1990–91	Ed Belfour	First	Goalie
	Chris Chelios	Second	Defense
1992–93	Ed Belfour	First	Goalie
	Chris Chelios	First	Defense
1994–95	Chris Chelios	First	Defense
	Ed Belfour	Second	Goalie
1995–96	Chris Chelios	First	Defense
1996–97	Chris Chelios	Second	Defense
2009–10	Patrick Kane	First	Right Wing
	Duncan Keith	First	Defense

Bobby Hull was named to the NHL All-Star Team 12 times, ten as a member of the First Team.

Chicago has hosted four NHL All-Star Games, each a memorable celebration of the game's best players:

2nd NHL All-Star Game
Chicago Stadium, November 3, 1948

Although the host team should have been the Cup-winning Maple Leafs, Chicago was promised the game because Blackhawks president Bill Tobin had been instrumental in organizing the inaugural event the previous year.

As well, the game during this era generally was played during the pre-season, but the 1948 event was held three weeks after the start of the regular season. As a result, players were in top condition and were so thoroughly entrenched in their team's efforts it was difficult for the All-Stars to come together as one.

Nevertheless, there was an extraordinary moment in the second period when Toronto defenseman Gus Mortson dropped the gloves with Gordie Howe. To this day it remains the only fight in All-Star Game history.

On the scoreboard, all the goals came in that testy middle period, the All-Stars getting three of the four to win the game, 3–1, in front of 12,794 fans at the Chicago Stadium.

15th NHL All-Star Game
Chicago Stadium, October 7, 1961

A record crowd of 14,534 took in the game, which featured the reigning Stanley Cup champion Blackhawks playing the best from the rest of the league. Incredibly, the only player who was in this game and who had been in the 1948 game in Chicago was none other than Mr. Hockey, Gordie Howe.

But the biggest cheer on the evening went to the home team's goalie, Glenn Hall, who received a three-minute standing ovation during introductions. "I was afraid I was going to burst out crying," he said after the game. "It was marvelous considering that there were so many truly great players on the ice tonight. If that kind of greeting doesn't make me play better, I doubt if anything ever will."

The All-Stars prevailed, 3–1, but Hall was sensational in goal, stopping 32 of 35 shots.

Opening ceremonies for the 1991 All-Star Game.

27th NHL All-Star Game
Chicago Stadium, January 29, 1974

By this time the League had altered the format so that the game featured only All-Stars and no Cup-champion team. It was East versus West in the now 16-team League, and every team had at least one player at the game.

Although the West won, 6–4, the game had a new wrinkle in that unlimited overtime was adopted in case of a tie. The East scored the only two goals of the first while the West had all three in the second. The West went up 5–2 early in the third and then held off a furious comeback attempt by the East.

The East's line of Norm Ullman, Yvan Cournoyer, and Frank Mahovlich was the best trio in the game, but their efforts weren't enough, as the West won before a delighted crowd of 16,426 at the Stadium.

Chicago goalie Tony Esposito (left) and Philadelphia goalie Bernie Parent share a laugh with Joan Rivers at the festivities prior to the 1974 All-Star Game at the Chicago Stadium.

Stan Mikita fools around during the Old-Timers' Game at the 1991 All-Star Game.

42nd NHL All-Star Game
Chicago Stadium, January 19, 1991

In a League that was now 22 teams strong, it was the Wales Conference versus the Campbell Conference in the All-Star Game. The Campbell side, which featured Blackhawks defenseman Chris Chelios and forwards Jeremy Roenick and Steve Larmer, prevailed in a wild game by an 11–5 score.

Toronto forward Vinecnt Damphousse was named MVP of the game thanks to four goals, three of which came in a nine-minute stretch of the final period to salt away the victory.

This marked the last All-Star Game at Chicago Stadium before the Blackhawks moved into the United Center, and it remains the last time the city has hosted the "glitter game."

Players

Sid Abel (1969)
Ed Belfour (2011)
Doug Bentley (1964)
Max Bentley (1966)
George Boucher (1960)
Frank Brimsek (1966)
Billy Burch (1974)
Lionel Conacher (1994)
Roy Conacher (1998)
Art Coulter (1974)
Cecil "Babe" Dye (1970)
Phil Esposito (1984)
Tony Esposito (1988)
Bill Gadsby (1970)
Charles Gardiner (1945)
Doug Gilmour (2011)
Michel Goulet (1998)
Glenn Hall (1975)
George Hay (1958)
Bobby Hull (1983)
Dick Irvin (1958)
Gordon "Duke" Keats (1958)
Hugh Lehman (1958)
Ted Lindsay (1966)
Harry Lumley (1980)
Duncan MacKay (1952)
Stan Mikita (1983)
Howie Morenz (1945)
Bill Mosienko (1965)
Bert Olmstead (1985)
Bobby Orr (1979)
Pierre Pilote (1975)
Denis Savard (2000)
Earl Seibert (1963)
Clint Smith (1991)
Allan Stanley (1981)
John Stewart (1964)
Harry Watson (1994)

Builders

Al Arbour (1996)
Tommy Ivan (1974)
John Mariucci (1985)
Fred McLaughlin (1963)
James D. Norris (1962)
James E. Norris (1958)
Rudy Pilous (1985)
Bud Poile (1990)
Art Wirtz (1971)
Bill Wirtz (1976)

Denis Savard was inducted into the Hockey Hall of Fame in 2000 in large part for his incredible years with the Blackhawks.

No.	Player	Date of Retiring
1	**Glenn Hall**	November 20, 1998
3	**Pierre Pilote**	November 12, 2008
3	**Keith Magnuson**	November 12, 2008
9	**Bobby Hull**	December 18, 1993
18	**Denis Savard**	March 19, 1998
21	**Stan Mikita**	October 19, 1980
35	**Tony Esposito**	November 20, 1998

Pierre Pilote and the late Keith Magnuson had their number 3 co-retired in a ceremony on November 12, 2008.

CONN SMYTHE TROPHY

2010	Jonathan Toews
2013	Patrick Kane

HART MEMORIAL TROPHY

1946	Max Bentley
1954	Al Rollins
1965	Bobby Hull
1966	Bobby Hull
1967	Stan Mikita
1968	Stan Mikita

ART ROSS TROPHY

1943	Doug Bentley
1946	Max Bentley
1947	Max Bentley
1949	Roy Conacher
1960	Bobby Hull
1962	Bobby Hull
1964	Stan Mikita
1965	Stan Mikita
1966	Bobby Hull
1967	Stan Mikita
1968	Stan Mikita

JAMES NORRIS MEMORIAL TROPHY

1963	Pierre Pilote
1964	Pierre Pilote
1965	Pierre Pilote
1982	Doug Wilson
1993	Chris Chelios
1996	Chris Chelios
2010	Duncan Keith

FRANK J. SELKE TROPHY

1986	Troy Murray
1991	Dirk Graham
2013	Jonathan Toews

CALDER MEMORIAL TROPHY

1936	Mike Karakas
1938	Carl Dahlstrom
1955	Ed Litzenberger
1960	Bill Hay
1970	Tony Esposito
1983	Steve Larmer
1991	Ed Belfour
2008	Patrick Kane

LADY BYNG MEMORIAL TROPHY

1936	Elwyn "Doc" Romnes
1943	Max Bentley
1944	Clint Smith
1945	Bill Mosienko
1964	Ken Wharram
1965	Bobby Hull
1967	Stan Mikita
1968	Stan Mikita

VEZINA TROPHY

1932	Chuck Gardiner
1934	Chuck Gardiner
1935	Lorne Chabot
1963	Glenn Hall
1967	Glenn Hall/ Dennis DeJordy
1970	Tony Esposito
1972	Tony Esposito/ Gary Smith
1974	Tony Esposito (shared with Bernie Parent, Philadelphia)
1991	Ed Belfour
1993	Ed Belfour

WILLIAM M. JENNINGS TROPHY

1991	Ed Belfour
1993	Ed Belfour/ Jimmy Waite
1995	Ed Belfour
2013	Corey Crawford/ Ray Emery

BILL MASTERTON MEMORIAL TROPHY

1970	Pit Martin
2004	Bryan Berard

JACK ADAMS AWARD

1983	Orval Tessier

LESTER PATRICK TROPHY

1967	James Norris
1969	Bobby Hull
1972	James D. Norris
1975	Tommy Ivan
1976	Stan Mikita
1978	Bill Wirtz
1985	Art Wirtz

Jonathan Toews was awarded the Conn Smythe Trophy winner for his sensational performance during the 2010 Stanley Cup Playoffs.

1963

5	Art Hampson
11	Wayne Davidson
16	Bill Carson

1964

4	Richie Bayes
10	Jan Popiel
16	Carl Hadfield
22	Moe L'Abbe

1965

2	Andy Culligan
7	Brian McKenney

1966

3	Terry Caffery
9	Ron Dussiaume
15	Larry Gibbons
21	Brian Morenz

1967

7	Bob Tombari

1968

9	John Marks

1969

13	Jean-Pierre Bordeleau
24	Larry Romanchych
36	Milt Black
48	Darryl Maggs
60	Mike Baumgartner
71	Dave Hudson

1970

14	Dan Maloney
28	Michel Archambault
42	Len Frig
56	Walt Ledingham
70	Gilles Meloche

1971

12	Dan Spring
26	Dave Kryskow
40	Bob Peppler
54	Clyde Simon
68	Dean Blais
82	Jim Johnston

1972

13	Phil Russell
29	Brian Ogilvie
45	Mike Veisor
61	Tom Peluso
77	Rejean Giroux
93	Rob Palmer
109	Terry Smith
125	Billy Reay
141	Gary Donaldson

1973

13	Darcy Rota
29	Reg Thomas
45	Randy Holt
61	Dave Elliott
77	Dan Hinton
93	Garry Doerksen
109	Wayne Dye
125	Jim Koleff
140	Jack Johnson
141	Steve Alley
156	Rick Clubbe
165	Gene Strate

1974

16	Grant Mulvey
34	Alain Daigle
52	Bob Murray
70	Terry Ruskowski
88	Dave Logan
106	Bob Volpe
124	Eddie Mio
141	Mike St. Cyr
158	Stephen Colp
173	Rick Fraser
188	Jean Bernier
200	Dwane Byers
210	Glen Ing

1975

7	Greg Vaydik
25	Daniel Arndt
43	Mike O'Connell
61	Pierre Giroux
76	Bob Hoffmeyer
97	Tom Ulseth
115	Ted Bulley
133	Paul Jensen

1976

9	Real Cloutier
27	Jeff McDill
45	Thomas Gradin
64	Dave Debol
81	Terry McDonald
99	John Peterson
115	John Rothstein

1977

6	Doug Wilson
19	Jean Savard
60	Randy Ireland
78	Gary Platt
96	Jack O'Callahan
114	Floyd Lahache
129	Jeff Geiger
144	Stephen Ough

1978

10	Tim Higgins
29	Doug Lecuyer
46	Rick Paterson
63	Brian Young
79	Mark Murphy
96	Dave Feamster
113	Dave Mancuso
130	Sandy Ross
147	Mark Locken
164	Glenn Van
179	Darryl Sutter

1979

7	Keith Brown
28	Tim Trimper
49	Bill Gardner
70	Lou Begin
91	Lowell Loveday
112	Doug Crossman

1980

3	Denis Savard
15	Jerome Dupont
28	Steve Ludzik
30	Ken Solheim
36	Len Dawes
57	Troy Murray
58	Marcel Frere
67	Carey Wilson
78	Brian Shaw
99	Kevin Ginnell
120	Steve Larmer
141	Sean Simpson
162	Jim Ralph
183	Don Dietrich
204	Dan Frawley

1981

12	Tony Tanti
25	Kevin Griffin
54	Darrell Anholt
75	Perry Pelensky
96	Doug Chessell
117	Bill Schafhauser
138	Marc Centrone
159	Johan Mellstrom
180	John Benns
201	Sylvain Roy

1982

7	Ken Yaremchuk
28	Rene Badeau
49	Tom McMurchy
70	Bill Watson
91	Brad Beck
112	Mark Hatcher
133	Jay Ness
154	Jeff Smith
175	Phil Patterson
196	Jim Camazzola
217	Mike James
238	Bob Andrea

1983

18	Bruce Cassidy
39	Wayne Presley
59	Marc Bergevin
79	Tarek Howard
99	Kevin Robinson
115	Jari Torkki
119	Mark LaVarre
139	Scott Birnie
159	Kent Paynter
179	Brian Noonan
199	Dominik Hasek
219	Steve Pepin

1984

3	Ed Olczyk
45	Trent Yawney
66	Tom Eriksson
90	Timo Lehkonen
101	Darin Sceviour
111	Chris Clifford
132	Mike Stapleton
153	Glenn Greenough
174	Ralph DiFiori
194	Joakim Persson
215	Bill Brown
224	David Mackey
235	Dan Williams

1985

11	Dave Manson
53	Andy Helmuth
74	Dan Vincelette
87	Rick Herbert
95	Brad Belland
116	Jonas Heed
137	Victor Posa
158	John Reid
179	Richard Laplante
200	Brad Hamilton
221	Ian Pound
242	Richard Braccia

1986

14	Everett Sanipass
35	Mark Kurzawski
77	Frantisek Kucera
98	Lonnie Loach
119	Mario Doyon
140	Mike Hudson
161	Marty Nanne
182	Geoff Benic
203	Glenn Lowes
224	Chris Thayer
245	Sean Williams

1987

8	Jimmy Waite
29	Ryan McGill
50	Cam Russell
60	Mike Dagenais
92	Ulf Sandstrom
113	Mike McCormick
134	Stephen Tepper
155	John Reilly
176	Lance Werness
197	Dale Marquette
218	Bill LaCouture
239	Mike Lappin

1988

8	Jeremy Roenick
50	Trevor Dam
71	Stefan Elvenes
92	Joe Cleary
113	Justin Lafayette
134	Craig Woodcroft
155	Jon Pojar
176	Matt Hentges
197	Daniel Maurice
218	Dirk Tenzer
239	Andreas Lupzig

1989

6	Adam Bennett
27	Mike Speer
48	Bob Kellogg
111	Tommi Pullola
132	Tracy Egeland
153	Milan Tichy
174	Jason Greyerbiehl
195	Matt Saunders
216	Mike Kozak
237	Mike Doneghey

1990

16	Karl Dykhuis
37	Ivan Droppa
79	Chris Tucker
121	Brent Stickney
124	Derek Edgerly
163	Hugo Belanger
184	Owen Lessard
205	Erik Peterson
226	Steve Dubinsky
247	Dino Grossi

1991

22	Dean McAmmond
39	Mike Pomichter
44	Jamie Matthews
66	Bobby House
71	Igor Kravchuk
88	Zac Boyer
110	Maco Balkovec
112	Kevin St. Jacques
132	Jacques Auger
154	Scott Kirton
176	Roch Belley
198	Scott MacDonald
220	Alexander Andrijevski
242	Mike Larkin
264	Scott Dean

1992

12	Sergei Krivokrasov
36	Jeff Shantz
41	Sergei Klimovich
89	Andy MacIntyre
113	Tim Hogan
137	Gerry Skrypec
161	Mike Prokopec
185	Layne Roland
209	David Hymovitz
233	Richard Raymond

1993

24	Eric Lecompte
50	Eric Manlow
54	Bogdan Savenko
76	Ryan Huska
90	Eric Daze
102	Patrick Pysz
128	Jonni Vauhkonen
180	Tom White
206	Sergei Petrov
232	Mike Rusk
258	Mike McGhan
284	Tom Noble

1994

14	Ethan Moreau
40	Jean-Yves Leroux
85	Steve McLaren
118	Marc Dupuis
144	Jim Ensom
170	Tyler Prosofsky
196	Mike Josephson
222	Lubomir Jandera
248	Lars Weibel
263	Rob Mara

1995

19	Dmitri Nabokov
45	Christian Laflamme
71	Kevin McKay
82	Chris Van Dyk
97	Pavel Kriz
146	Marc Magliarditi
149	Marty Wilford
175	Steve Tardif
201	Casey Hankinson
227	Michael Pittman

1996

31	Remi Royer
42	Jeff Paul
46	Geoff Peters
130	Andy Johnson
184	Mike Vellinga
210	Chris Twerdun
236	Andrei Kozyrev

1997

13	Daniel Cleary
16	Ty Jones
39	Jeremy Reich
67	Michael Souza
110	Ben Simon
120	Pete Gardiner
130	Kyle Calder
147	Heath Gordon
174	Jared Smith
204	Sergei Shikhanov
230	Chris Feil

1998

8	Mark Bell
94	Matthias Trattnig
156	Kent Huskins
158	Jari Viuhkola
166	Jonathan Pelletier
183	Tyler Arnason
210	Sean Griffin
238	Alexandre Couture
240	Andrei Yershov

1999

23	Steve McCarthy
46	Dmitri Levinsky
63	Stepan Mokhov
134	Michael Jacobsen
165	Michael Leighton
194	Mattias Wennerberg
195	Yorick Treille
223	Andrew Carver

2000

10	Mikhail Yakubov
11	Pavel Vorobiev
49	Jonas Nordquist
74	Igor Radulov
106	Scotty Balan
117	Olli Malmivaara
151	Alexander Barkunov
177	Mike Ayers
193	Joey Martin
207	Cliff Loya
225	Vladislav Luchkin
240	Adam Berkhoel
262	Peter Flache
271	Reto Von Arx
291	Arne Ramholt

2001

9	Tuomo Ruutu
29	Adam Munro
59	Matt Keith
73	Craig Anderson
104	Brent MacLellan
115	Vladimir Gusev
119	Alexei Zotkin
142	Tommi Jaminki
174	Alexander Golovin
186	Petr Puncochar
205	Teemu Jaaskelainen
216	Oleg Minakov
268	Jeff Miles

2002

21	Anton Babchuk
54	Duncan Keith
93	Alexander Kozhevnikov
128	Matt Ellison
156	James Wisniewski
188	Kevin Kantee
219	Tyson Kellerman
251	Jason Kostadine
282	Adam Burish

2003

14	Brent Seabrook
52	Corey Crawford
59	Michal Barinka
151	Lasse Kukkonen
156	Alexei Ivanov
181	Johan Andersson
211	Mike Brodeur
245	Dustin Byfuglien
275	Michael Grenzy
282	Chris Porter

2004

3	Cam Barker
32	Dave Bolland
41	Bryan Bickell
45	Ryan Garlock
54	Jakub Sindel
68	Adam Berti
120	Mitch Maunu
123	Karel Hromas
131	Trevor Kell
140	Jake Dowell
165	Scott McCulloch
196	Petri Kontiola
214	Troy Brouwer
223	Jared Walker
229	Eric Hunter
256	Matthew Ford
260	Marko Anttila

2005

7	Jack Skille
43	Mike Blunden
54	Dan Bertram
68	Evan Brophey
108	Niklas Hjalmarsson
113	Nathan Davis
117	Denis Istomin
134	Brennan Turner
167	Joe Fallon
188	Joe Charlebois
203	Adam Hobson

2006

3	Jonathan Toews
33	Igor Makarov
61	Simon Danis-Pepin
76	Tony Lagerstrom
95	Ben Shutron
96	Joe Palmer
156	Jan-Mikael Juutilainen
169	Chris Auger
186	Peter LeBlanc

2007

1	Patrick Kane
38	Bill Sweatt
56	Akim Aliu
69	Maxime Tanguay
86	Josh Unice
126	Joe Lavin
156	Richard Greenop

2008

11	Kyle Beach
68	Shawn Lalonde
132	Teigan Zahn
162	Jonathan Carlsson
169	Ben Smith
179	Braden Birch
192	Joe Gleason

2009

28	Dylan Olsen
59	Brandon Pirri
89	Daniel Delisle
119	Byron Froese
149	Marcus Kruger
177	David Pacan
195	Paul Phillips
209	David Gilbert

2010

24	Kevin Hayes
35	Ludvig Rensfeldt
54	Justin Holl
58	Kent Simpson
60	Stephen Johns
90	Joakim Nordstrom
120	Rob Flick
151	Mirko Hofflin
180	Nick Mattson
191	Macmillan Carruth

2011

18	Mark McNeill
26	Phillip Danault
36	Adam Clendening
43	Brandon Saad
70	Michael Paliotta
79	Klas Dahlbeck
109	Maxim Shalunov
139	Andrew Shaw
169	Sam Jardine
199	Alexander Broadhurst
211	Johan Mattsson

2012

18	Teuvo Teravainen
48	Dillon Fournier
79	Chris Calnan
139	Garret Ross
149	Travis Brown
169	Vincent Hinostroza
191	Brandon Whitney
191	Matt Tomkins

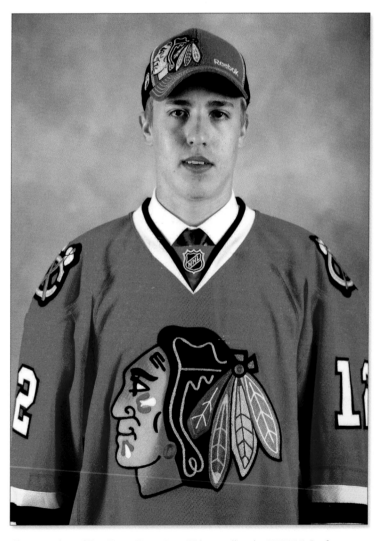

Chicago selected Finn Teuvo Teravainen 18th overall at the 2012 NHL Draft.

L to R: Three of Chicago's greatest – Ken Wharram, Stan Mikita, and Bobby Hull.

BRYAN BICKELL

Born: Bowmanville, Ontario, March 9, 1986

Left Wing—shoots left

6'4"

223 lbs.

Drafted 41st overall by Chicago in 2004

A career Blackhawk, Bickell signed his first contract (a three-year deal) with Chicago in 2006 after four years in the OHL with Ottawa 67's and Windsor Spitfires.

Bickell started his professional career in the AHL with Norfolk Admirals in the 2006–07 season. His first taste of NHL action came when he was called up to the Blackhawks on April 5, 2007. He scored a goal in his NHL debut that night, a 3–2 win over Detroit, but he spent most of the first four years of his pro career in the minor leagues with the Rockford IceHogs. He was recalled more than a dozen times during those developmental seasons, sometimes not dressing, other times getting in a few games, and he was used by coach Joel Quenneville as insurance during the 2010 playoffs.

Bickell's career changed once and for all at training camp in 2010 after the Cup win. At 24, with several pro seasons under his belt, he became a regular for the first time. He responded by scoring 17 goals in what amounted to his rookie season. But this was just the tip of the iceberg. If there was one great surprise from the Blackhawks run to the Cup in 2013, it was Bickell's performance.

He played with an extra level of grit and determination, raised his game to a new level, and justified his presence on the team's top line alongside Jonathan Toews and Patrick Kane. Indeed, as his two linemates sometimes struggled to deal with tight checking, Bickell thrived. He scored three goals in the first round of the 2013 playoffs, two the second round, and three again in the third round to lead the team.

Career Statistics	Regular Season					Playoffs				
	GP	G	A	P	Pim	GP	G	A	P	Pim
2006–07 CHI	3	2	0	2	0	DNQ				
2007–08 CHI	4	0	0	0	2	DNQ				
2008–09 CHI	DNP					DNP				
2009–10 CHI	16	3	1	4	5	4	0	1	1	2
2010–11 CHI	78	17	20	37	40	5	2	2	4	0
2011–12 CHI	71	9	15	24	48	6	2	0	2	4
2012–13 CHI	48	9	14	23	25	for 2013 playoff stats see p. 18				
NHL Totals	220	40	50	90	120					

for 2013 playoff stats see p. 18

DAVE BOLLAND

Born: Mimico, Ontario, June 5, 1986	
Center—shoots right	
6′	
181 lbs.	
Drafted 32nd overall by Chicago in 2004	

Another lifelong member of the Blackhawks, Dave Bolland has developed pretty much as Chicago had hoped, and for that the team has been extremely happy. He was only 23 years old when he won the Cup with Chicago in 2010 and, incredibly, had as many points in those playoffs as he had during the regular season.

Bolland had an excellent junior career in the OHL. In four years with the London Knights he developed steadily, helping the team to a Memorial Cup in 2004–05 while leading the playoffs with 15 goals in as many games. That performance earned him a spot on the World Junior team in 2006 where he, and teammate Jonathan Toews, won gold. He wrapped up his last season (2005–06) in the OHL by posting a league-leading 57 goals, as well as placing second in points (130).

Bolland then moved on to the Norfolk Admirals where he played most of the first two years of his professional career. He got his first call up to the NHL on October 25, 2006, and the next year he played in 39 games. In 2008, he earned a permanent spot on the big team out of training camp and went on to record an impressive 19 goals.

Midway through 2009–10 Bolland required back surgery and missed nearly half the season. He returned in time for the playoffs and provided dependable two-way play and secondary scoring for the Blackhawks Cup run. Healthy again for the 2010–11 season, he continued to play intelligent hockey for coach Joel Quenneville and has become a steady presence on the Blackhawks' checking line.

Career Statistics	Regular Season					Playoffs				
	GP	G	A	P	Pim	GP	G	A	P	Pim
2006–07 CHI	1	0	0	0	0	DNQ				
2007–08 CHI	39	4	13	17	28	DNQ				
2008–09 CHI	81	19	28	47	52	17	4	8	12	24
2009–10 CHI	39	6	10	16	28	22	8	8	16	30
2010–11 CHI	61	15	22	37	34	4	2	4	6	4
2011–12 CHI	76	19	18	37	47	6	0	3	3	2
2012–13 CHI	35	7	7	14	22	for 2013 playoff stats see p. 18				
NHL Totals	332	70	98	168	211	49	14	23	37	60

for 2013 playoff stats see p. 18

BRANDON BOLLIG

Born: St. Charles, Montana, January 31, 1987

Left Wing—shoots left

6'2"

223 lbs.

Signed as a free agent by Chicago on April 3, 2010

Not many players can lay claim to making their NHL debuts on Leap Day, February 29, but Brandon Bollig is one such example. He dressed for an NHL game for the first time on that date in 2012, against Toronto, and played 5:34, registering two shots on goal over the course of his eight shifts. He was called up from the AHL and became a valuable addition after the Blackhawks traded John Scott to the Rangers.

Bollig spent two years at St. Lawrence University but was undrafted. He was signed by Chicago after his final NCAA season in the spring of 2010 and assigned to Rockford in the AHL. He has spent most of the last three year with the IceHogs, but he played 18 games for the Blackhawks last year and made the team, more or less, from training camp in January this year.

Bollig's one and only NHL goal to date came during the 2012 playoffs against Phoenix, but Chicago isn't looking for him to put the puck in the net. Rather, he is there to look after his teammates and create a little skating room for the star forwards, a thankless job outside the dressing room but a valuable one to those who understand the pressures of the assignment.

Career Statistics	Regular Season					Playoffs				
	GP	G	A	P	Pim	GP	G	A	P	Pim
2011-12 CHI	18	0	0	0	58	4	1	0	1	19
2012-13 CHI	25	0	0	0	51	for 2013 playoff stats see p. 18				
NHL Totals	43	0	0	0	109	4	1	0	1	19

SHELDON BROOKBANK

Born: Lanigan, Saskatchewan, October 3, 1980

Defenseman—shoots right

6'1"

202 lbs.

Signed as a free agent by Chicago on July 1, 2012

Without question Sheldon Brookbank is the kind of player who has "piece of the puzzle" written all over him. When he signed with the Blackhawks as a free agent last summer, it was a calculated move by both general manager Stan Bowman and Brookbank himself.

Now 32 years old, he has been around the league long enough to develop a certain kind of reputation. A team knows up front what it's going to get with him; a defenseman who can kill penalties and move the puck up ice well. Big and strong, Brookbank is most obviously a stay-at-home defenseman with a variegated skill set.

Brookbank is responsible and not flashy. He won't go end-to-end with the puck – but he won't make many errors in his own end either. Never drafted, he worked his way to the NHL through sheer force of will, starting in provincial hockey in Saskatchewan, moving to the ECHL and AHL over six years, and finally making his NHL debut with Nashville in 2006–07, the same season he was named the AHL's best defenseman.

After moving to New Jersey and Anaheim, Brookbank was a free agent in the summer of 2012, and for the first time in his career he had options. He had proven himself as a solid player and saw quickly that the Blackhawks would be a good fit, as did GM Bowman. The day of free agency, July 1, 2012, the two met and agreed to a two-year deal.

Career Statistics	Regular Season					Playoffs				
	GP	G	A	P	Pim	GP	G	A	P	Pim
2006–07 NSH	3	0	1	1	12	DNP				
2007–08 NJ	44	0	8	8	63	DNP				
2008–09 NJ	15	0	0	0	25	—	—	—	—	—
2008–09 ANA	29	1	3	4	51	13	0	0	0	18
2009–10 ANA	66	0	9	9	114	DNP				
2010–11 ANA	40	0	0	0	63	4	0	0	0	14
2011–12 ANA	80	3	11	14	72	DNP				
2012-13 CHI	26	1	0	1	21	for 2013 playoff stats see p. 18				
NHL Totals	303	5	32	37	421	17	0	0	0	32

DANIEL CARCILLO

Born: King City, Ontario, January 28, 1985

Left Wing—shoots left

6′

205 lbs.

Drafted 73rd overall by Pittsburgh in 2003

A tough guy, to be sure, Daniel Carcillo can also play the game when given a chance, as he has proved along the way in his NHL career. He started his junior career with Sarnia in the OHL, and after turning pro in 2006 he was sent to Pittsburgh's AHL affiliate in Wilkes-Barre.

Carcillo was traded a year and a half later to Phoenix before ever playing with the Penguins. The following year he was a full-time member of the team. He led the NHL in penalty minutes in 2007–08 and, in one memorable game on April 4, 2008, he also scored a hat trick, a feat not many enforcers can lay claim to.

Near the trading deadline the following year Carcillo was sent on to Philadelphia, and it was here he found a solid home. He again piled up the penalty minutes, but he was never a detriment to the team because of poor penalties. The highlight of his time with the Flyers came in game three of the team's first-round playoff matchup against New Jersey. Carcillo scored the overtime winner to give Philadelphia a 2–1 series lead, and they went on to win in five games.

In the 2010 Cup Final, coach Peter Laviolette inserted him into the lineup for Game 3 to give the team some spark, and he did just that, helping the Flyers get back in the series with a crucial 4–3 win in overtime.

After one more season with the Flyers Carcillo signed with Chicago. The one-year contract had only 28 games in it as things turned out when Carcillo suffered a serious ACL injury. The Hawks signed him to a two-year extension a little later, though, and he has been with Chicago ever since.

Career Statistics	Regular Season					Playoffs				
	GP	G	A	P	Pim	GP	G	A	P	Pim
2006–07 PHX	18	4	3	7	74	DNQ				
2007–08 PHX	57	13	11	24	324	DNQ				
2008–09 PHX	54	3	7	10	174	—	—	—	—	—
2008–09 PHI	20	0	4	4	80	5	1	1	2	5
2009–10 PHI	76	12	10	22	207	17	2	4	6	34
2010–11 PHI	57	4	2	6	127	11	2	1	3	30
2011–12 CHI	28	2	9	11	82	DNP				
2012–13 CHI	23	2	1	3	11	for 2013 playoff stats see p. 18				
NHL Totals	333	40	47	87	1,079	33	5	6	11	69

COREY CRAWFORD

Born: Montreal, Quebec, December 31, 1984

Goalie—catches left

6'2"

208 lbs.

Drafted 52nd overall by Chicago in 2003

The Corey Crawford story is one of perseverance and patience, loyalty and mutual support – and it has a happy ending. The Montreal native played four seasons in the QMJHL during which time he was drafted by the Blackhawks. After graduating from junior, he was assigned to Norfolk in the AHL where he spent most of the next two years.

He made his NHL debut on January 22, 2006, in relief of Adam Munro, but had just one more game with Chicago before being sent back to the AHL. When the Blackhawks moved their affiliate from Norfolk to Rockford, Crawford maintained his role as number-one man on the farm, playing only occasionally with the big club over the next two seasons.

By the time the 2010–11 season started he was nearly 26, had played only nine NHL games, and looked destined to be a minor leaguer or, at best, a backup. Over the years the Blackhawks had Antti Niemi, Cristobal Huet, and Marty Turco all in net, but they had departed and left an opening for Crawford to prove himself. He pounced.

Crawford played in 57 games in each of the next two years, but despite his solid play still competed with the equally capable Ray Emery for the number-one job. Emery was very capable, but he pushed Crawford to be better, and in 2012–13, it was Crawford who established himself not only as the go-to goalie but also one of the best in the league.

The Crawford–Emery tandem, in fact, allowed the fewest goals this past season and won the William Jennings Trophy as a result, and the Blackhawks' deep playoff run in 2013 is in large part thanks to the play of "Crow." The goalie may have had a slow start to his career, but he was faithful to the Hawks and they to him, and now the team has a superstar puckstopper and Crawford has a full-time job.

Career Statistics	Regular Season						Playoffs					
	GP	W–L–T	Mins	GA	SO	GAA	GP	W–L	Mins	GA	SO	GAA
2005–06 CHI	2	0–0–0	86	5	0	3.48			DNP			
2007–08 CHI	5	1–2–0	224	8	1	2.14			DNP			
2008–09 CHI			DNP				1	0–0	16	1	0	3.75
2009–10 CHI	1	0–1–0	59	3	0	3.04			DNP			
2010–11 CHI	57	33–18–6	3,337	128	4	2.30	7	3–4	435	16	1	2.21
2011–12 CHI	57	30–17–7	3,218	146	0	2.72	6	2–4	396	17	0	2.58
2012–13 CHI	30	19–5–5	1,761	57	3	1.94	for 2013 playoff stats see p. 18					
NHL Totals	152	83–43–19	8,685	347	8	2.40	14	5–8	847	34	1	2.41

RAY EMERY

Born: Hamilton, Ontario, September 28, 1982

Goalie—catches left

6'2"

196 lbs.

Drafted 99th overall by Ottawa in 2001

Draft day 2001 seems like a million miles away now for Ray Emery, who has led a flashy and colorful life in hockey, starred in the NHL, played in the KHL, and returned to triumph against all odds.

The Blackhawks had a record-setting start to their 2012–13 season by going 24 games without a defeat. Emery was 12–0–0 to start the season, a record for a perfect start by a goalie. But his journey from childhood in Hamilton to record-breaker in Chicago was no straight line.

As a kid, he couldn't make any team, but when he finally settled in with Sault Ste. Marie in the OHL, he knew he had found his calling. He was drafted by Ottawa in 2001 and then had a superb year with the Greyhounds, leading the OHL in games played and wins and being named the best junior goalie in Canada.

Still, it took Emery three years to become a full-time goalie in the NHL. The first two years he played mostly in Binghamton, Ottawa's AHL affiliate, but he did get called up for a few games in the NHL with the Senators. Emery was at his best in the 2007 playoffs when the team went to the Final, only to lose to Anaheim in five games.

After being released by the Senators Emery played a year in Russia. He matured and continued to improve as a goalie, and when he made it clear he wanted to play in the NHL for 2009–10, the Flyers gave him a second chance he coveted dearly.

Emery's strong play in his return to the NHL was cut short in December 2009. He had been the team's number-one goalie, but a serious abdomen injury forced him to the press box for the rest of the year. He played with Anaheim the next year, then the Blackhawks gave him a tryout at camp in 2011. They signed him to a one-year deal which they renewed the next year. Together with Corey Crawford, he was awarded the William M. Jennings Trophy at the end of the 2012–13 season.

Career Statistics	Regular Season						Playoffs					
	GP	W–L–T	Mins	GA	SO	GAA	GP	W–L	Mins	GA	SO	GAA
2002–03 OTT	3	1–0–0	85	2	0	1.41	DNP					
2003–04 OTT	3	2–0–0	126	5	0	2.38	DNP					
2005–06 OTT	39	23–11–4	2,168	102	3	2.82	10	5–5	604	29	0	2.88
2006–07 OTT	58	33–16–6	3,351	138	5	2.47	20	13–7	1,249	47	3	2.26
2007–08 OTT	31	12–13–4	1,689	88	0	3.13	DNP					
2009–10 PHI	29	16–11–1	1,684	74	3	2.64	DNP					
2010–11 ANA	10	7–2–0	527	20	0	2.28	6	2–3	319	17	0	3.20
2011–12 CHI	34	15–9–4	1,774	83	0	2.81	DNP					
2012–13 CHI	21	17–1–0	1,116	36	3	1.94	for 2013 playoff stats see p. 18					
NHL Totals	228	126–63–19	12,520	548	14	2.63	36	20–15	2,172	93	3	2.57

MICHAEL FROLIK

Born: Kladno, Czechoslovakia (Czech Republic),
February 17, 1988

Right Wing—shoots left

6'1"

198 lbs.

Drafted 10th overall by Florida in 2006

It didn't take long for Michael Frolik to make the move from his native Czech Republic to North America. As soon as the 18-year-old was drafted by Florida in 2006, he packed his bags and made his way to Canada to play junior hockey in Quebec.

Frolik played for Rimouski for two years in the QMJHL where he quickly became likened to legendary countryman Jaromir Jagr. Not quite as tall or strong, he had a similar style in that he shielded the puck well and had great touch around the goal. During these two seasons he also played for the Czechs at the U20 Worlds, scoring a total of nine goals in 12 games.

After two seasons in the "Q," Frolik attended the Panthers' training camp in 2008 and never looked back. Adjusting to the bigger, faster, and stronger NHL seemed of little consequence to Frolik. He had 21 goals in each of his first two seasons.

Midway through the 2010–11 season he was traded to Chicago. The deal saw Frolik and Alexander Salak go to the Blackhawks while Florida acquired Jack Skille and Hugh Jessiman. In his two and a half seasons in Chicago, Frolik's production has slowed down. Nevertheless, he is a skilled forward who has won a bronze medal in each of the last two World Championships.

Frolik has played only three seasons of playoff hockey, yet already holds a record. He has scored two penalty shots in the playoffs – one in 2011, the other in 2013 – the only player to have done so in the game's long history.

Career Statistics	Regular Season					Playoffs				
	GP	G	A	P	Pim	GP	G	A	P	Pim
2008–09 FLA	79	21	24	45	22	DNQ				
2009–10 FLA	82	21	22	43	43	DNQ				
2010–11 FLA	52	8	21	29	16	—	—	—	—	—
2010–11 CHI	28	3	6	9	14	7	2	3	5	2
2011–12 CHI	63	5	10	15	22	4	2	1	3	0
2012–13 CHI	45	3	7	10	8	for 2013 playoff stats see p. 18				
NHL Totals	349	61	90	151	125	11	4	4	8	2

MICHAL HANDZUS

Born: Banska Bystrica, Czechoslovakia (Slovakia), March 11, 1977

Center—shoots left

6'5"

215 lbs.

Drafted 101st overall by St. Louis in 1995

A 36-year-old from Slovakia, Michal Handzus has been here, there, and everywhere during his nearly two decades of pro hockey, including two stints with the Blackhawks. He developed in his native Slovakia for two years after being drafted by St. Louis, and then the Blues assigned him to their farm team in Worcester for the 1997–98 season.

A year later, he was on the team that included two other prominent Slovakians, Pavol Demitra, and Lubos Bartecko. But after only two and a half years in St. Louis, Handzus was traded to Phoenix, the first of several changes of scenery he would experience in the coming decade and more. It was really when he got to Philadelphia in 2002 at age 25 that he started to blossom into the player many scouts thought he could be.

In the summer of 2006, though, he was traded to Chicago for Kyle Calder. Just eight games into his career as a Blackhawk he tore his ACL causing him to miss the remainder of the season. He signed with Los Angeles as a free agent the following summer.

After stops in California with the Kings and Sharks, Handzus returned to the Windy City late in the 2012–13 season. He was traded by San Jose on April 1, 2013, for a 4th-round draft choice, and while the Sharks were eliminated in the playoffs by Los Angeles, Handzus and the Hawks went all the way.

Internationally, Handzus had his greatest moment in 2002, playing on the Slovakian team that won gold at the World Championship, the first and greatest moment of glory for the young nation.

Career Statistics	Regular Season					Playoffs				
	GP	G	A	P	Pim	GP	G	A	P	Pim
1998–99 STL	66	4	12	16	30	11	0	2	2	8
1999–00 STL	81	25	28	53	44	7	0	3	3	6
2000–01 STL	36	10	14	24	12	—	—	—	—	—
2000–01 PHX	10	4	4	8	21			DNQ		
2001–02 PHX	79	15	30	45	34	5	0	0	0	2
2002–03 PHI	82	23	21	44	46	13	2	6	8	6
2003–04 PHI	82	20	38	58	82	18	5	5	10	10
2005–06 PHI	73	11	33	44	38	6	0	2	2	2
2006–07 CHI	8	3	5	8	6			DNP		
2007–08 LA	82	7	14	21	45			DNQ		
2008–09 LA	82	18	24	42	32			DNQ		
2009–10 LA	81	20	22	42	38	6	3	2	5	4
2010–11 LA	82	12	18	30	20	6	1	1	2	0
2011–12 SJ	67	7	17	24	18	2	0	0	0	0
2012–13 SJ	28	1	1	2	12	—	—	—	—	—
2012–13 CHI	11	1	5	6	4		for 2013 playoff stats see p. 18			
NHL Totals	950	181	286	467	482	74	11	21	32	38

NIKLAS HJALMARSSON

Born: Eksjo, Sweden, June 6, 1987

Defenseman—shoots left

6'3"

205 lbs.

Drafted 108th overall by Chicago in 2005

Now 26 years old and in the prime of his career, Niklas Hjalmarsson has been a career Blackhawk through the first eight years of his hockey life. When Chicago drafted him at age 18 in 2005, the team believed he could develop into a Borje Salming–type player; that is, talented with the puck and not afraid of a physical game without it. The years have proved the scouts correct.

Hjalmarsson remained in Sweden for two years after being drafted in 2005, not coming to North America until the summer of 2007. He split his first two pro seasons between Chicago and the AHL affiliate in Rockford where he matured and developed seemingly every game. In 2009 he made the Chicago lineup as a full-time player and he has been a mainstay on the blue line ever since.

It was at the end of that first full season, 2009–10, that Hjalmarsson helped Chicago win the Cup. That summer, San Jose presented him with an offer sheet for a four-year contract worth $14 million, but the Blackhawks were quick to match it, knowing they could not afford to lose a defenseman of his caliber.

What Hjalmarsson proved in 2010 and again in 2013 is that as the games get bigger, so does the quality of his play. An intense player on a good day, he becomes a force when the chips are on the line. The team has no better shot-blocker, and he can play as many minutes in whatever situation as is required of him.

Career Statistics	Regular Season					Playoffs				
	GP	G	A	P	Pim	GP	G	A	P	Pim
2007–08 CHI	13	0	1	1	13	DNQ				
2008–09 CHI	21	1	2	3	0	17	0	1	1	6
2009–10 CHI	77	2	15	17	20	22	1	7	8	6
2010–11 CHI	80	3	7	10	39	7	0	2	2	2
2011–12 CHI	69	1	14	15	14	6	0	1	1	4
2012–13 CHI	46	2	8	10	22	for 2013 playoff stats see p. 18				
NHL Totals	306	9	47	56	108	52	1	11	12	18

MARIAN HOSSA

Born: Stara Lubovna, Czechoslovakia (Slovakia), January 12, 1979

Right Wing—shoots left

6'1"

210 lbs.

Drafted 12th overall by Ottawa in 1997

Now 34 years old and closer to the end of his career than the start, Marian Hossa continues to shine as one of the most skilled players in the game. His consistency, his skill, and more recently his determination to overcome a serious injury, all put him in a rare class among the best of the best.

He passed the magic 1,000-game mark this past season, and next season he can look forward to scoring his 500th career goal and 1,000th career point, all benchmarks of a player destined for the Hockey Hall of Fame. On the international scene, he has represented Slovakia with distinction for the better part of a decade and a half, including three Olympics and eight World Championships.

He spent his early career with Ottawa, the team that drafted him in 1997, establishing himself as one of the stars of the league. At the start of the 2006–07 season, Hossa signed with Atlanta where he thrived, registering 92 points his first year and then 100 points (including 43 goals) in 2006–07.

At the trade deadline in 2007–08, Hossa was moved to Pittsburgh where it was thought he would help lead the team to Stanley Cup glory. The Pens lost to the Red Wings that spring, and Hossa signed with his former rivals, Detroit, in the offseason, expecting a chance to be part of a winning team. The 2009 Stanley Cup Final featured a rematch of the year before, with Hossa again on the losing side as his former team beat Detroit in seven games.

On July 1, 2009, Hossa signed a contract with Chicago, believing he could help the Hawks win the Cup several times over. He made good on his contract that first year, winning the Cup in his third consecutive attempt.

Career Statistics	Regular Season					Playoffs				
	GP	G	A	P	Pim	GP	G	A	P	Pim
1997–98 OTT	7	0	1	1	0	DNP				
1998–99 OTT	60	15	15	30	37	4	0	2	2	4
1999–00 OTT	78	29	27	56	32	6	0	0	0	2
2000–01 OTT	81	32	43	75	44	4	1	1	2	4
2001–02 OTT	80	31	35	66	50	12	4	6	10	2
2002–03 OTT	80	45	35	80	34	18	5	11	16	6
2003–04 OTT	81	36	46	82	46	7	3	1	4	0
2005–06 ATL	80	39	53	92	67	DNQ				
2006–07 ATL	82	43	57	100	49	4	0	1	1	6
2007–08 ATL	60	26	30	56	30	—	—	—	—	—
2007–08 PIT	12	3	7	10	6	20	12	14	26	12
2008–09 DET	74	40	31	71	63	23	6	9	15	10
2009–10 CHI	57	24	27	51	18	22	3	12	15	25
2010–11 CHI	65	24	32	57	32	7	2	4	6	2
2011–12 CHI	81	29	48	77	20	3	0	0	0	0
2012–13 CHI	40	17	14	31	16	for 2013 playoff stats see p. 18				
NHL Totals	1,018	434	501	935	544	130	36	61	97	73

PATRICK KANE

Born: Buffalo, New York, November 19, 1988	
Right Wing—shoots left	
5'10"	
178 lbs.	
Drafted 1st overall by Chicago in 2007	

Young, talented, and grown since he first broke into the league, Patrick Kane is now one of the game's elite players who has proved his ability to raise his game as the stakes get bigger. Of course, no finer example of his skills can be cited than his overtime goals in Game 6 of the 2010 Stanley Cup Final to give Chicago its first Cup in 49 years. But before then and since, he has proved himself again and again.

By the time he was 22, Kane had already played in all four levels of international hockey: U18, U20, World Championship, and the Olympics. Kane was the 1st-overall draft choice in 2007 after an outstanding junior career. He was part of the U.S. National Team Development Program for two years (2004–06), winning gold at the U18 in 2006. Kane then played for the London Knights in the 2006–07 season, leading the OHL with 145 points and winning rookie of the year. He also played for USA at the 2007 U20, earning a bronze medal.

In 2007, Kane was invited to his first training camp with the Blackhawks. He made the team and led the rookie scoring race with 72 points, earning him the Calder Trophy, beating out teammate Jonathan Toews and Washington's Nicklas Backstrom.

Kane has played mostly on a line with captain Toews over the years. The two faced off against each other in the gold-medal game of the 2010 Olympics, won by Canada, but in Chicago the two are a compatible and deadly pair. Toews is generally the passer and Kane the finisher.

Their combination in the 2013 playoffs brought the Hawks to their second Final in four years. In the Conference Final against Los Angeles, Kane had a hat trick, including the winner in the second period of overtime, to eliminate the Kings, Toews assisting on two of the goals. It was Kane's second career playoff hat trick.

Career Statistics	Regular Season					Playoffs				
	GP	G	A	P	Pim	GP	G	A	P	Pim
2007–08 CHI	82	21	51	72	52	DNQ				
2008–09 CHI	80	25	45	70	42	16	9	5	14	12
2009–10 CHI	82	30	58	88	20	22	10	18	28	6
2010–11 CHI	73	27	46	73	28	7	1	5	6	2
2011–12 CHI	82	23	43	66	40	6	0	4	4	10
2012–13 CHI	47	23	32	55	8	for 2013 playoff stats see p. 18				
NHL Totals	446	149	275	424	190	51	20	32	52	30

DUNCAN KEITH

Born: Winnipeg, Manitoba, July 16, 1983
Defenseman—shoots left
6'1"
194 lbs.
Drafted 54th overall by Chicago in 2002

Duncan Keith was born in Winnipeg, spent his early years in Fort Frances, Ontario, and lived as a teen in Penticton, British Columbia where he played for the Penticton Panthers of the BCHL. At age 18 he moved to Michigan to play for the State University and continued his path to the NHL. It was there, in 2002, that Keith was drafted by the Blackhawks.

He played only a year and a half at MSU before moving home and continuing his career in junior hockey with the Kelowna Rockets. After just half a season in the WHL the Blackhawks assigned him to their AHL farm team for the start of the 2003–04 season. He spent two full years developing into a reliable defenseman in the minors, finally debuting with Chicago to start the 2005–06 season.

After his rookie year, Chicago signed Keith to a five-year contract extension, but they had even bigger things in mind once they saw how great a player he was. In December 2009, they tore up this contract and drafted a new one, ensuring he'd be with the team for a long time to come.

Keith logs big minutes on the ice, often playing more than 23:00 a game. He's earned this ice time by being a reliable player, in 2012–13 he was among the top 25 in plus/minus through the regular season and continued that trend into the playoffs.

In addition to his exceptional play, Keith is a work-horse game in, game out, and his resilience is rare. Since entering the league in 2005, he has missed only 15 games in eight seasons, an admirable show of consistency few players can match.

Career Statistics	Regular Season					Playoffs				
	GP	G	A	P	Pim	GP	G	A	P	Pim
2005–06 CHI	81	9	12	21	79	DNQ				
2006–07 CHI	82	2	29	31	76	DNQ				
2007–08 CHI	82	12	20	32	56	DNQ				
2008–09 CHI	77	8	36	44	60	17	0	6	6	10
2009–10 CHI	82	14	55	69	51	22	2	15	17	10
2010–11 CHI	82	7	38	45	22	7	4	2	6	6
2011–12 CHI	74	4	36	40	42	6	0	1	1	2
2012–13 CHI	47	3	24	27	31	for 2013 playoff stats see p. 18				
NHL Totals	607	59	250	309	103	52	6	24	30	28

MARCUS KRUGER

Born: Stockholm, Sweden, May 27, 1990

Center—shoots left

6'

181 lbs.

Drafted 149th overall by Chicago in 2009

One of four Swedes on the team, Marcus Kruger is still in the developmental stages of his career. He played pro as early as 2007 with Djurgardens, and during his first two seasons made a favorable impression with Chicago scouts, who encouraged general manager Stan Bowman to draft him in 2009.

Kruger elected to stay in Sweden for two more years, but the Blackhawks played him in seven NHL games late in the season 2010–11 season to give him a taste of the speed and skill of the league. He had led the Swedes to a bronze medal at the 2010 U20 World Championship, where he had six assists in as many games.

After his NHL call-up, Kruger returned to Sweden, and a few weeks later he played at the senior World Championship in Slovakia. He had two goals in nine games, and Tre Kronor won a silver medal. By the fall of 2011, he was big, strong, and mature enough to play in the NHL on a regular basis.

The 2011–12 season was his first full season of pro in North America. Kruger played the entire season with the Hawks, but after an early playoff exit he accepted a second invitation to play at the World Championship, in Helsinki and Stockholm.

Kruger's first career goal in the playoffs was a big one. On May 9, he scored what turned out to be the game winner in a 5–1 victory over Minnesota in Game 5 of the Conference Quarterfinals, the win eliminating the Wild and taking the Hawks to the next round.

Career Statistics	Regular Season					Playoffs				
	GP	G	A	P	Pim	GP	G	A	P	Pim
2010–11 CHI	7	0	0	0	4	5	0	1	1	0
2011–12 CHI	71	9	17	26	22	6	0	0	0	0
2012–13 CHI	47	4	9	13	24	for 2013 playoff stats see p. 18				
NHL Totals	125	13	26	39	50	11	0	1	1	0

for 2013 playoff stats see p. 18

NICK LEDDY

Born: Eden Prairie, Minnesota, March 20, 1991

Defenseman—shoots left

6'

191 lbs.

Drafted 16th overall by Minnesota in 2009

One of the bright young American prospects, Nick Leddy is the kind of stud defensemen who could turn out to be the mainstay of Chicago's blue line for years to come. He attended Eden Prairie High School in Minnesota, a prep school known for its hockey program, and he even declined to go to Ann Arbor, Michigan, to join the U.S. National Team Development Program, which would have given him a better opportunity to play at the U18 World Championships. As it was, he attended U18 camp but didn't make the final team.

Nonetheless, Leddy was drafted by the Wild, after which he attended the University of Minnesota. Midway through his freshman year he represented Team USA at the U20 in Saskatoon, where the team won a bronze medal. A month later, the Hawks acquired his rights when the Wild traded Leddy and roster player Kim Johnsson for Cam Barker.

Soon after the Hawks signed Leddy to an entry-level contract, making no bones about the fact they believed he was NHL-ready. Leddy left U of M at season's end and turned pro in the summer of 2011. He divided his first year between the Blackhawks and Rockford and then played all 82 games with the big club a year after.

In 2012–13, he played the full season, developing as Chicago had hoped into an impressive defenseman who can skate, provide offense, and be a leader among the blue line corps.

Career Statistics	Regular Season					Playoffs				
	GP	G	A	P	Pim	GP	G	A	P	Pim
2010–11 CHI	46	4	3	7	4	7	0	0	0	0
2011–12 CHI	82	3	34	37	10	6	1	2	3	0
2012–13 CHI	48	6	12	18	10	for 2013 playoff stats see p. 18				
NHL Totals	176	13	49	62	24	13	1	2	3	0

JAMAL MAYERS

Born: Toronto, Ontario, October 24, 1974

Right Wing—shoots right

6'1"

222 lbs.

Drafted 89th overall by St. Louis in 1993

Jamal Mayers isn't just the oldest player on the Blackhawks, he is also one of the oldest in the league, having been drafted exactly two decades ago. He started his career with four years at Western Michigan University, and it was after his freshman season that he was selected by St. Louis in the draft.

Mayers remained at WMU until he earned his degree, after which the Blues assigned him to their farm team in Worcester. Mayers appeared in six games with the big club in 1996–97 but spent most of the next two years in the minors. Once he was recalled midway through the 1998–99 season, though, his days in the minors were over.

He spent his first decade of pro hockey with St. Louis, but the day before the 2008 draft he was traded to Toronto. Just a year and a half later, the Leafs included him in a blockbuster deal in which Matt Stajan, Niklas Hagman, Ian White, and Mayers were traded to Calgary for Dion Phaneuf, Keith Aulie, and Fredrik Sjostrom.

Mayers elected to become a free agent at the end of the 2009–10 season and signed a one-year contract with San Jose over the summer, leaving the Flames after just 27 games. A similar fate played out the next summer when he signed a new deal with Chicago.

Despite limited playoff success, Mayers has played for Canada at the World Championship on three occasions. In 2000, Canada finished fourth, but a few years later, in 2007, Mayers won gold and went to the gold-medal game the next year in Quebec City before settling with a silver.

He has made a career out of being a dependable and responsible forward, not flashy but never a detriment. In many respects, he's a coach's dream, and teammates love him because, as the saying goes, he plays for the name on the front of the sweater, not the back.

Career Statistics	Regular Season					Playoffs				
	GP	G	A	P	Pim	GP	G	A	P	Pim
1996–97 STL	6	0	1	1	2	DNQ				
1998–99 STL	34	4	5	9	40	11	0	1	1	8
1999–00 STL	79	7	10	17	90	7	0	4	4	2
2000–01 STL	77	8	13	21	117	15	2	3	5	8
2001–02 STL	77	9	8	17	99	10	3	0	3	2
2002–03 STL	15	2	5	7	8	DNP				
2003–04 STL	80	6	5	11	91	5	0	0	0	0
2005–06 STL	67	15	11	26	129	DNQ				
2006–07 STL	80	8	14	22	89	DNQ				
2007–08 STL	80	12	15	27	91	DNQ				
2008–09 TOR	71	7	9	16	82	DNQ				
2009–10 TOR	44	2	6	8	78	—	—	—	—	—
2009–10 CAL	27	1	5	6	53	DNQ				
2010–11 SJ	78	3	11	14	124	12	0	0	0	12
2011–12 CHI	81	6	9	15	91	3	0	0	0	0
2012–13 CHI	19	0	2	2	16	for 2013 playoff stats see p. 18				
NHL Totals	915	90	129	219	1,200	63	5	8	13	32

JOHNNY ODUYA

Born: Stockholm, Sweden, October 1, 1981

Defenseman—shoots left

6'

190 lbs.

Drafted 221st overall by Washington in 2001

The 31-year-old Johnny Oduya has had a long and peripatetic life in hockey that began back in his native Sweden with Hammarby. In 2000, though, in an effort to get noticed by NHL scouts and learn the North American game, Oduya moved to Canada and played junior in Quebec, first with Moncton and later Victoriaville. After his first season the Washington Capitals used a low draft choice to acquire his rights, but still only 19 he didn't feel ready for the NHL.

After two years of junior in the "Q," Oduya moved back to Sweden and played for Hammarby again, moving his way up to the Elitserien where he played for three years. The Capitals never signed him, and once he became a free agent, New Jersey took an interest in him, offering him a contract in the fall of 2006.

Now 25, Oduya felt ready to give North American hockey a try. His timing couldn't have been better. Several defensemen were injured during training camp, and he made the Devils. Making the most of his opportunity, he played a physical and uncomplicated game, quickly establishing himself as an NHL-caliber player.

Indeed, Oduya played three and a half seasons with New Jersey, missing only a few games because of injury. On February 4, 2010, however, he was traded to Atlanta with Niclas Bergfors, Patrice Cormier, and a

1st-round draft choice in a huge deal which saw the Devils acquire Ilya Kovalchuk and Anssi Salmela.

Two weeks later, Oduya was wearing the colors of Tre Kronor at the Vancouver Olympics where Sweden finished a disappointing fifth. It was Oduya's second international competition. He had helped the Swedes win a bronze medal at the 2009 World Championship in Switzerland.

Oduya signed with Winnipeg in the summer of 2011, but midway through the season he was traded to Chicago for two draft choices in 2013. He has given the Blackhawks much needed depth on the blue line and has proved his worth as a smart defensive player with and without the puck.

Career Statistics	Regular Season					Playoffs				
	GP	G	A	P	Pim	GP	G	A	P	Pim
2006–07 NJ	76	2	9	11	61	6	0	1	1	6
2007–08 NJ	75	6	20	26	46	5	0	1	1	6
2008–09 NJ	82	7	22	29	30	7	0	0	0	2
2009–10 NJ	40	2	2	4	18	—	—	—	—	—
2009–10 ATL	27	1	8	9	12			DNQ		
2010–11 ATL	82	2	15	17	22			DNQ		
2011–12 WIN	63	2	11	13	33	—	—	—	—	—
2011–12 CHI	18	1	4	5	0	6	0	3	3	0
2012–13 CHI	48	3	9	12	10		for 2013 playoff stats see p. 18			
NHL Totals	511	26	100	126	232	24	0	5	5	14

MICHAL ROZSIVAL

Born: Vlasim, Czechoslovakia (Czech Republic), September 3, 1978

Defenseman—shoots right

6'1"

212 lbs.

Drafted 105th overall by Pittsburgh in 1996

An impressive defenseman who has been around the block, Michal Rozsival is the kind of player any team needs if it is going to win. Strong, solid, reliable, he started his pro career in 1996 as soon as he was drafted while still only 17 years old.

Rozsival moved to Canada to play junior, with Swift Current in the Western Hockey League, and over the course of the next two years he got to develop and understand the North American game. In fact, he was voted the WHL's best defenseman in his second season. The Penguins then assigned him to Syracuse in the AHL for the 1998–99 season after which he was clearly ready for the NHL.

If there was a problem with Rozsival's early career, it was injuries. He missed nearly 30 games in 2002–03 with various ailments, and 2003–04 was a complete write off. He missed the entire season with a serious knee injury. The next year, during the lockout, he returned home to the Czech Republic to play.

He signed with the Rangers when the NHL started up again and put together his best string of years.

Rozsival missed only ten games over the next five years, and the Rangers went to the playoffs four of those seasons, albeit with limited success. He later signed with Phoenix before being wooed to Chicago in the summer of 2012.

In many ways, the veteran defenseman has been a perfect addition to Stan Bowman's team. Rozsival can log plenty of ice time and can adapt, literally, shift to shift with new defense partners. He can play the power play or, more likely, kill penalties, and is adept at getting the puck out of his own end. Not flashy, he is a piece of the puzzle on the blue line without which Cups can't be won.

Career Statistics	Regular Season					Playoffs				
	GP	G	A	P	Pim	GP	G	A	P	Pim
1999–00 PIT	75	4	17	21	48	2	0	0	0	4
2000–01 PIT	30	1	4	5	26	DNQ				
2001–02 PIT	79	9	20	29	47	DNQ				
2002–03 PIT	53	4	6	10	40	DNQ				
2005–06 NYR	82	5	25	30	90	4	0	1	1	8
2006–07 NYR	80	10	30	40	52	10	3	4	7	10
2007–08 NYR	80	13	25	38	80	10	1	5	6	10
2008–09 NYR	76	8	22	30	52	7	0	0	0	4
2009–10 NYR	82	3	20	23	78	DNQ				
2010–11 NYR	32	3	12	15	22	—	—	—	—	—
2010–11 PHX	33	3	3	6	20	4	0	0	0	2
2011–12 PHX	54	1	12	13	34	15	0	0	0	2
2012–13 CHI	27	0	12	12	14	for 2013 playoff stats see p. 18				
NHL Totals	783	64	208	272	603	52	4	10	14	40

for 2013 playoff stats see p. 18

BRANDON SAAD

Born: Pittsburgh, Pennsylvania, October 27, 1992

Left Wing—shoots left

6'1"

202 lbs.

Drafted 43rd overall by Chicago in 2011

Brandon Saad has a bright future ahead in the NHL if his bright past is any indication. He was born in Mario Lemieux country, just months after Super Mario captained the Penguins to their second straight Stanley Cup, and was identified early in his teen years by USA Hockey as a talent to watch.

Saad spent the 2009–10 season with the U.S. National Team Development Program in Ann Arbor, Michigan, and during that season he played for the U.S. at the U18 World Championship, helping his team beat Sweden, 3–1, in the gold-medal game.

Realizing he was close to attaining his dream of playing in the NHL, Saad then decided to play junior hockey in the OHL rather than play NCAA hockey. He played two seasons with Saginaw, the second as team captain, and he proved valuable in all areas of the game. He could score, play sound defensive hockey, and, of course, was a leader.

After his first year of junior Saad was drafted by the Hawks and attended training camp that fall. He made enough of an impression that he played his first two NHL games at the start of the season before being returned to the OHL for further development.

Saad played for the U.S. again in 2012 at the U20 World Championship in Calgary and Edmonton, and was assigned to Rockford to start the 2012–13 season. The half season in the AHL did wonders for his development, and when the NHL season started, he made the big club.

He made such an impression league-wide that he was nominated for the Calder Trophy along with Brendan Gallagher of Montreal and Jonathan Huberdeau of Florida.

Career Statistics	Regular Season					Playoffs				
	GP	G	A	P	Pim	GP	G	A	P	Pim
2011–12 CHI	2	0	0	0	0	2	0	1	1	0
2012–13 CHI	46	10	17	27	12	for 2013 playoff stats see p.				
NHL Totals	48	10	17	27	12	2	0	1	1	0

BRENT SEABROOK

Born: Richmond, British Columbia, April 20, 1985

Defenseman—shoots right

6'3"

218 lbs.

Drafted 14th overall by Chicago in 2003

A Blackhawks defenseman through the first eight years of his NHL career, Brent Seabrook and Duncan Keith have formed arguably the best tandem in the league over the much of that time. Big and tough, he takes care of things in his end while Keith is the more offensive-minded of the two.

Seabrook was drafted by the Blackhawks 14th overall in 2003 after leading Canada to a gold medal at the World U18 Championship. It would still be two years before he made it to the NHL, but in the meantime he played well for the Lethbridge Hurricanes of the WHL and played with Team Canada at the World Junior Championship, winning a silver and gold medal in 2004 and 2005, respectively.

Seabrook has been a mainstay on the Blackhawks blue line since making the team out of training camp in 2005. For much of that time, he has been paired with Keith, together shutting down the top lines in the NHL. Although he is blessed with some ability in the offensive zone, he is known more for his superb work inside his own blue line, limiting scoring chances and moving the puck up ice quickly and effectively.

That being said, his career highlight with the puck might well have come in Game 7 of the Conference Semifinals in 2013 against Detroit. The Hawks fell behind in the series 3–1 but won the next two games to force a final and deciding match. That went into overtime, and it was Seabrook who scored the game and series winner in the fourth period to complete the amazing comeback.

Career Statistics	Regular Season					Playoffs				
	GP	G	A	P	Pim	GP	G	A	P	Pim
2005–06 CHI	69	5	27	32	60	DNQ				
2006–07 CHI	81	4	20	24	104	DNQ				
2007–08 CHI	82	9	23	32	90	DNQ				
2008–09 CHI	82	8	18	26	62	17	1	11	12	14
2009–10 CHI	78	4	26	30	59	22	4	7	11	14
2010–11 CHI	82	9	39	48	47	5	0	1	1	6
2011–12 CHI	78	9	25	34	22	6	1	2	3	0
2012–13 CHI	47	8	12	20	23	for 2013 playoff stats see p. 18				
NHL Totals	599	56	190	246	467	50	6	21	27	34

PATRICK SHARP

Born: Winnipeg, Manitoba, December 27, 1981

Forward—shoots right

6'1"

199 lbs.

Drafted 95th overall by Philadelphia in 2001

Although the 31-year-old Patrick Sharp was drafted by Philadelphia and played the first two and a half years of his NHL career with the Flyers, Sharp is every bit a lifelong Blackhawks forward who has the character and personality Chicago fans expect of their heroes.

Indeed, after Jonathan Toews and Patrick Kane, Sharp is likely the team's most important player on offense. He is reliable and consistent, and when the going gets tough, he remains as effective as ever; a player whom opponents can't just shut down through tougher checking.

Sharp was not always the star. Far from it. He went unnoticed in the NHL Entry Draft and so went to the University of Vermont for two years (2000–02) during which time he was finally noticed by the Flyers. In 2001 at age 19, they drafted him. In 2002, he left college to start a pro career that developed impressively.

It took Sharp three years of AHL play before he made it to the NHL on a full-time basis. Even so, 22 games through his first full season the Flyers traded him to Chicago in what looked like a minor deal. He and Eric Meloche headed to the Blackhawks and the Flyers got a 3rd-round draft choice in 2006.

Sharp scored 20 goals in his first full season with Chicago and 36 the next year, establishing himself as a star of the Blackhawks' offense. He was at his best in the 2010 playoffs when he averaged a point a game through the 22-game grind that took Chicago to their first Cup since 1961, and he had his best year statistically the next year when he had 34 goals and 71 points. That summer of 2011 he signed a five-year contract extension that will keep him in Chicago until 2017.

Most important, Sharp is so versatile and valuable that if teams manage to shut down Toews and Kane, they will be leaving Sharp free to contribute – and he will do just that. He might play in the shadow of the two younger stars, but they realize his play is as vital to victory as their own. Opponents ignore him at their peril.

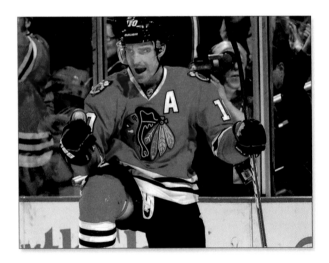

Career Statistics	Regular Season					Playoffs				
	GP	G	A	P	Pim	GP	G	A	P	Pim
2002–03 PHI	3	0	0	0	2	DNP				
2003–04 PHI	41	5	2	7	55	12	1	0	1	2
2005–06 PHI	22	5	3	8	10	—	—	—	—	—
2005–06 CHI	50	9	14	23	36	DNQ				
2006–07 CHI	80	20	15	35	74	DNQ				
2007–08 CHI	80	36	26	62	55	DNQ				
2008–09 CHI	61	26	18	44	41	17	7	4	11	6
2009–10 CHI	82	25	41	66	28	22	11	11	22	16
2010–11 CHI	74	34	37	71	38	7	3	2	5	2
2011–12 CHI	74	33	36	69	38	6	1	0	1	4
2012–13 CHI	28	6	14	20	14	for 2013 playoff stats see p. 18				
NHL Totals	595	199	206	405	391	64	23	17	40	30

ANDREW SHAW

Born: Belleville, Ontario, July 20, 1991

Right Wing—shoots right

5'11"

180 lbs.

Drafted 139th overall by Chicago in 2011

A mid-round draft choice by the Blakchawks two years ago, Shaw is a gritty and determined forward with nothing but upside at this early stage of his career. He played his junior hockey with the Niagara IceDogs and later the Owen Sound Attack, winning the OHL championship in 2011 and leading all scorers with seven points in the Memorial Cup that spring.

Shaw split his rookie season of pro between Chicago and Rockford, recording identical totals with both teams. He made his NHL debut on January 5, 2012, scoring a goal on his first shot, against Ilya Bryzgalov of the Flyers. It was no fluke, either. Shaw had the puck behind the Flyers' goal and came quickly out front, made a great move around defenseman Kimmo Timonen, and then stuffed a high backhand past Bryzgalov.

"I was nervous coming into the game," Shaw said after. "But once the puck dropped, it's another game of hockey. It was great to get that first one out of the way."

Shaw played the game on the top line with Jonathan Toews and Patrick Sharp, replacing Daniel Carcillo. Some 35 friends and family drove down from Belleville, Ontario, for the game

Shaw split his time between the minors and NHL again in 2012–13, but he gained valuable experience and has worked his way nicely into coach Joel Quenneville's lineup.

Career Statistics	Regular Season					Playoffs				
	GP	G	A	P	Pim	GP	G	A	P	Pim
2011–12 CHI	37	12	11	23	50	3	0	0	0	15
2012–13 CHI	48	9	6	15	38	for 2013 playoff stats see p 18				
NHL Totals	85	21	17	38	88	3	0	0	0	15

VIKTOR STALBERG

Born: Gothenburg, Sweden, January 17, 1986

Right Wing—shoots left

6'3"

209 lbs.

Drafted 161st overall by Toronto in 2006

The fact that a Swede made it to the NHL is nothing special. Indeed, Sweden provides the league more players than any other European nation. But what is surprising is the path Stalberg took to get to North America's top league.

After only one season with Frolunda in Sweden's junior league he was drafted by the Maple Leafs in the summer of 2006. But rather than stay at home to develop or move to Canada to play junior, Stalberg decided to play college hockey in the U.S., an extremely difficult challenge because of academic requirements and the need to speak excellent English.

These were only small obstacles for Stalberg, who joined the University of Vermont in the fall of 2006. He played with the Catamounts for three years, after which the Leafs signed him to an entry-level contract. Stalberg was immediately sent to the AHL for the end of the season, and in 2009–10 he split his time between the NHL's Leafs and the AHL's Marlies.

After only one season Stalberg was traded to the Blackhawks in a multi-player deal in which he, Philippe Paradis, and Chris DiDomenico went to Chicago and Kris Versteeg and Bill Sweatt went to the Leafs.

Stalberg blossomed with the Hawks, scoring 12 goals in his first full season and nearly doubling that to 22 a year later. When the Hawks were eliminated in the first round of the 2012 playoffs, Stalberg was invited to play for Sweden at the World Championship in Stockholm, an offer he quickly accepted.

Career Statistics	Regular Season					Playoffs				
	GP	G	A	P	Pim	GP	G	A	P	Pim
2009–10 TOR	40	9	5	14	30	DNQ				
2010–11 CHI	77	12	12	24	43	7	1	0	1	5
2011–12 CHI	79	22	21	43	34	6	0	2	2	8
2012–13 CHI	47	9	14	23	25	for 2013 playoff stats see p. 18				
NHL Totals	243	52	52	104	132	13	1	2	3	13

JONATHAN TOEWS

Born: Winnipeg, Manitoba, April 29, 1988

Center—shoots left

6'2"

210 lbs.

Drafted 3rd overall by Chicago in 2006

They call him "Captain Serious," a compliment which drives him crazy because he wants to be known as more laid back than he is. In truth, no one brings the focused energy to the arena better than Jonathan Toews, only 25 years old with a career's-worth of experience and success already on his resume.

When he led the Hawks to their Stanley Cup win in 2010, Toews became the youngest member in the history of the Triple Gold Club. He had won Olympic gold only months earlier, and he won World Championship gold with Canada in 2007 soon after his 18th birthday. Earlier that season he won his second gold medal at the U20 World Championship, thus becoming the first Canadian to win gold at the World Junior and senior Championships in the same season.

What is more amazing is that Toews has been a leader for every event he's won. He was named Conn Smythe Trophy winner for his amazing 2010 Cup playoffs, the Best Forward by the IIHF Directorate at the 2010 Olympics, and made the All-Star Team at the 2007 U20s.

After being drafted 3rd overall by Chicago in 2006, Toews finished his second year at North Dakota and then joined the Blackhawks as a rookie for the 2007–08 season at age 20. On October 10, 2007, Toews scored a goal on his first shot in his first NHL game and went on to record points in his first ten NHL games, the second-longest such streak in league history.

Since then, "Captain Serious" has made the team his. He leads by example on ice and off, and even if he is having a bad game he is contributing in other ways – blocking shots, winning key faceoffs, setting up linemates. Toews is among that group of superstar players who will be the face of the league for another decade and more, and there is no doubt he will add to his trophy case even after this second Cup victory.

Career Statistics	Regular Season					Playoffs				
	GP	G	A	P	Pim	GP	G	A	P	Pim
2007–08 CHI	64	24	30	54	44	DNQ				
2008–09 CHI	82	34	35	69	51	17	7	6	13	26
2009–10 CHI	76	25	43	68	47	22	7	22	29	4
2010–11 CHI	80	32	44	76	26	7	1	3	4	2
2011–12 CHI	59	29	28	57	28	6	2	2	4	6
2012–13 CHI	47	23	25	48	27	for 2013 playoff stats see p. 18				
NHL Totals	408	167	205	372	223	52	17	33	50	38

for 2013 playoff stats see p. 18

COACH JOEL QUENNEVILLE

Born: Windsor, Ontario, September 15, 1958

Few men in the game today have enjoyed dual careers as player and coach for as long as has Joel Quenneville. A Toronto Maple Leafs draft choice in 1978, he played in the NHL for 13 years and has now been coaching for the better part of 16.

As a player, Quenneville was known as a stay-at-home defenseman. He played for five teams but never had a chance to raise the Stanley Cup. Quenneville's last season as a player was his first as a coach. In 1991–92, he was a playing coach with the St. John's Maple Leafs, Toronto's AHL affiliate, and soon after he was named head coach of the Springfield Indians.

Quenneville served as an assistant coach in Quebec and later Colorado during the team's move from Canada to Denver, helping the team to victory in the 1996 Stanley Cup Final.

In 1996, Quenneville was hired by the St. Louis Blues as head coach, and over the next eight seasons he became the most successful coach in team history, compiling a record of 307–191–95. The team made the playoffs every full season, and in 1999–2000 he was named winner of the Jack Adams Trophy.

When the Blues got off to a slow start in 2003–04, he was fired, but he wasn't out of work for long. He was named head coach of Colorado in 2004, but after

three seasons he left the team and was hired as a scout for Chicago a few months later.

The start of the 2008–09 season was a crazy one in Chicago, though, and only four games in coach Denis Savard was fired and Quenneville was asked to step in. He immediately transformed the young team into an offensive, exciting juggernaut. The Hawks went to the Conference Final in 2009, and a year later they won it all.

Although the team made two quick playoff exits in 2011 and 2012, it was in large part because of significant player turnover after the Cup win. But Quenneville and GM Stan Bowman have now put the team in a strong position moving forward, and the fruits of their labors can be seen in this second Cup win in four years.

Team	Year	G	W	L	T	OTL	Pts	Playoffs
STL	1996–97	40	18	15	7	—	83	Lost in round 1
STL	1997–98	82	45	29	8	—	98	Lost in round 2
STL	1998–99	82	37	32	13	—	87	Lost in round 2
STL	1999–2000	82	51	19	11	1	114	Lost in round 1
STL	2000–01	82	43	22	12	5	103	Lost in round 3
STL	2001–02	82	43	27	8	4	98	Lost in round 2
STL	2002–03	82	41	24	11	6	99	Lost in round 1
STL	2003–04	61	29	23	7	2	91	Fired before playoffs
COL	2005–06	82	43	30	—	9	95	Lost in round 2
COL	2006–07	82	44	31	—	7	95	DNQ
COL	2007–08	82	44	31	—	7	95	Lost in round 2
CHI	2008–09	78	45	22	—	11	104	Lost in round 3
CHI	2009–10	82	52	22	—	8	112	Won Stanley Cup
CHI	2010–11	82	44	29	—	9	97	Lost in round 1
CHI	2011–12	82	45	26	—	11	101	Lost in round 1
CHI	2012–13	48	36	7	—	5	77	Won Stanley Cup
NHL Totals		1,211	660	389	77	74		

THE YEAR OF THE
CHICAGO BLACKHAWKS®

Acknowledgements

The author would like to thank the many people who have helped create what is hopefully a worthy testament to the 2013 Stanley Cup season in such a short time. First, to publisher Jordan Fenn of Fenn/M&S and to Kristin Cochrane at McClelland & Stewart Doubleday Canada Publishing Group. To the entire editorial team at M&S, notably editors Liz Kribs and Michael Melgaard as well as Janine Laporte, Carla Kean, Bhavna Chauhan, James Young, Ruta Liormonas, and those at Random House U.S. sales. To designer and typesetter Five Seventeen and Terra Page for managing text and images in quick and orderly, not to mention attractive, fashion. To Lucas Aykroyd and Carol Schram for assistance with research and writing the playoff game stories on short notice with shorter deadlines. To my agent Dean Cooke for sorting out the business side of things in a lucid and cogent manner. To Getty Images for granting easy access to their incomparable archive of images, past and present. And, lastly, to my own team of inspirational leaders, none of whom played on a broken leg or got stitched up at the end of the bench but were important all the same – Liz, Ian, Zac, and Emily, my mom, who never utters the word "hockey" without using "be careful," and my wife, Jane, who simply can't wait to see the Cup won every spring.

Photo Credits

All photos are courtesy of Getty Images.